The Feedback Process

The Feedback Process

*Engaging Students With
Meaningful Comments
About Their Writing*

Karen A. Wink

ROWMAN & LITTLEFIELD
Lanham • Boulder • New York • London

Published by Rowman & Littlefield
An imprint of The Rowman & Littlefield Publishing Group, Inc.
4501 Forbes Boulevard, Suite 200, Lanham, Maryland 20706
www.rowman.com

86-90 Paul Street, London EC2A 4NE, United Kingdom

Copyright © 2022 by Karen A. Wink

All rights reserved. No part of this book may be reproduced in any form or by any electronic or mechanical means, including information storage and retrieval systems, without written permission from the publisher, except by a reviewer who may quote passages in a review.

British Library Cataloguing in Publication Information Available

Library of Congress Cataloging-in-Publication Data

Names: Wink, Karen A., author.
Title: The feedback process : engaging students with meaningful comments about their writing / Karen A. Wink.
Description: Lanham, MD : Rowman & Littlefield, [2022] | Includes bibliographical references and index. | Summary: "Drawing from classroom research, The Feedback Process offers teaching methods for commenting on students' drafts-both in written and auditory formats. This book includes writing assignments, rubrics, surveys, and sample student papers with commentary from English and other humanities courses, as well as models for writing and audio-taping comments"—Provided by publisher.
Identifiers: LCCN 2022019207 (print) | LCCN 2022019208 (ebook) | ISBN 9781475864557 (cloth ; alk. paper) | ISBN 9781475864564 (paperback ; alk. paper) | ISBN 9781475864571 (epub)
Subjects: LCSH: English language—Composition and exercises—Study and teaching (Higher) | Academic writing—Study and teaching (Higher) | Feedback (Psychology) | English teachers—Training of.
Classification: LCC PE1404 .W549 2022 (print) | LCC PE1404 (ebook) | DDC 808/.0420711—dc23/eng/20220610
LC record available at https://lccn.loc.gov/2022019207
LC ebook record available at https://lccn.loc.gov/2022019208

I extend a debt of gratitude to my University of Maryland graduate professors, Dr. Jeanne Fahnestock, Dr. Joseph McCaleb, and Dr. Wayne Slater, who taught me to view the world rhetorically with all its splendid benefits; and for their patience, as it took me twenty-two years to finally write this book based on my doctoral dissertation. When I think of the top five people who have influenced me most as scholars and educators, they all rank in this group. Thanks to them, I know what it means to be an influential, critical-examining, and visionary professor. I extend further thanks to Dr. Faye Ringel and Nancy Dunker for their edits, wisdom, and mentorship throughout the years.

Contents

Preface		ix
Introduction		xi
1	The Feedback Process	1
2	Writing Assignments	13
3	Assessment	25
4	Rubrics	41
5	Commenting Vocabulary	49
6	Written Commentary	73
7	Audio Commentary	89
8	Emotional Component	115
9	Feedback on Feedback	137
10	Feed Forward	143

APPENDIXES

A	Terms of the Feedback Process	151
B	Case Study of Formative and Summative Online Comments for Half- and Final Drafts of Research Paper, Freshman English Composition Course	153

C	Case Study of Formative and Summative Online Comments for Rough and Final Drafts of Research Paper, Freshman History Course	169
D	Student Survey: Writing Practices and the Feedback Process	181

Bibliography	183
Index	187
About the Author	199

Preface

We all probably remember "stinging" feedback that we received from instructors—even years later. As an undergraduate, I took "Reporting I" to fulfill a requirement for a journalism minor. Since I was an English education major, I wrote the first paper in a style more suited to literature courses.

When I received my graded paper, my journalism professor had written a large "BS" across the front page. Needless to say, I was mortified, then annoyed as I had put forth a good-faith but apparently misguided effort. Although the passing of years has dimmed the sting, the event is still memorable.

We can all remember receiving little to no feedback from instructors after honest efforts to write various papers. In my graduate degree program, I remember writing my heart out on a paper, only to receive one word of feedback: "Elaborate." My head filled with questions: Where? How? To what extent? I was left unfulfilled, and the entire experience felt like a wasted opportunity.

My interest in studying commentary was born of frustration toward and puzzlement about this complex process—and I was determined to find ways to improve its efficiency in writing classrooms. As a high school teacher in Columbia, Maryland, I was dismayed when I wrote some useful comments that, ultimately, students misunderstood.

One example sums up this glaring disconnect. After returning rough drafts and ending my comments with "polish," a junior student approached me and indignantly asked, "Why did you write 'Polish' on my paper?" Dumbfounded, I corrected him and sent him away to revise or "polish" his paper. A series of these moments led me to my dissertation topic—"Matches and Mismatches in Teachers' Intentions and Students' Perceptions of Commentary"—at the University of Maryland.

Although twenty-two years have passed since I defended my dissertation (in which committee members confessed that they felt self-conscious commenting on my writing), I find the process of commenting just as challenging, as does every colleague with whom I have discussed the topic.

The Feedback Process: Engaging Students With Meaningful Comments About Their Writing combines my passions of psychology, writing, research, reading, and technology. Since 1999, I have studied my own practice of commentary, conducted classroom-based research on this topic, and presented findings at faculty in-services and English education conferences. The reaction is always curious and positive—and some are even surprised that a professor studies commentary.

With such demands on their time, instructors want practical, "classroom-tested" strategies; they want to know "what works." Through trial and error, I have learned the "best of" practices of approximately 80–85% of the feedback process. Why not 95–100%? It's that 15–20% uncontrollable factor—"head-shaking" moments similar to mine will always exist because we are all, well, human. I hope this text is accessible and useful in learning to communicate more productively with students to improve their writing.

Introduction

Welcome to an in-depth look at a dynamic part of our writing classrooms: feedback. I have written this text to present the best of what I have learned as an English professor through trial and error (and am still learning after twenty-seven years of teaching high school and college students). We are all in this together to examine a vigorous part of student-writing development.

We have important reasons to examine this crucial and time-consuming activity: First, feedback is "the most important or nearly the most important variable affecting the amount and quality of student learning" (Brookhart 2016, 1); and, secondly, "feedback has one of the highest effects on student learning," according to John Hattie, who synthesized more than eight hundred meta-analysis studies related to achievement including instructors' commentary on students' papers (2019, 2).

This research suggests an urgency to reexamine this central part of instructors' work. All writers, especially students, need feedback because their writing is meant to be understood by primary audiences rather than abstract audiences who are expected to read a robotic production of words, which results in an exercise in futility.

The feedback process has inherent issues that can lead to instructors' and students' mismatched intentions and perceptions in the revision process. Various reasons account for these mismatches. Sometimes, the language of comments is confusing. For example, contradictory comments such as "be more concise and develop," or "condense and elaborate" puzzle students, who often dismiss them. Sometimes students place little value on feedback—no matter how relevant and meaningful. Sometimes, they prioritize sentence-level corrective comments as a learning strategy because it is easier and avoids content comments altogether—or vice versa. Sometimes, instructors take ownership of the papers, causing students to lose their voices as they see their writing as a Legos pile of broken sentences that need to be fixed by instructors, not by them.

Therefore, students become discouraged, and instructors become frustrated. The result? Missed opportunities and hindered development of student writing. This text will address these issues by providing a practical handbook essentially to increase matches between instructors' intentions and students' perceptions.

Commenting on student drafts takes an inordinate amount of time, and the return on instructors' investment is not always profitable. They may spend 20–30 minutes per paper for 50–100+ students, which equates to numerous hours, leaving little room for class preparations or other duties. This is especially true when students write about diverse topics (e.g., research papers), so it takes dedicated effort to delve into each student's thinking. Taking longer than the norm, the tendency is to provide more feedback when the "less is more" philosophy should apply to this practice.

Overall, this text aims to shorten the time instructors spend commenting on the substantial number of papers every quarter or semester while still providing effective feedback.

Despite this research, "there is a great deal of evidence that students do not understand the feedback given by [instructors]" (Nicol and Macfarlane-Dick 210), which even extends to a global perspective: "contemporary students in tertiary institutions around the world are broadly dissatisfied with written feedback they received" (James, Krause, and Jennings 2010; Nicol 2010). These findings are sobering and seem to play out in humanities classrooms with not all but enough students.

During the feedback process, students may try to read comments but are unable to decipher their instructors' handwriting; they may become confused by instructors' intended meaning; and they may fall back into the default thinking that comments are only justification of grades from biased instructors (e.g., "My instructor is biased toward me, so she decided to give me a 'C' and only wrote comments to fit that grade").

Another college student explained, "I try to understand it [comments], but I seldom understand the written feedback on the assignments. Sometimes I get frustrated if I can't read their writing or understand what they are saying" (quoted in Adcroft 411). Providing comments online is one way to eliminate the issue of poor handwriting, and writing 3–4 major comments clearly (rather than innumerable ones unclearly) is also useful.

Another student, Jake, said, "I don't like when teachers hardly write any comments and give me a bad grade" (Interview). Students sometimes are left frustrated by comments (or lack thereof); therefore, they do not or cannot apply them in future drafts. Conversely, sometimes students misunderstand comments due to reading comprehension challenges and "not being sufficiently equipped [emotionally] to assimilate the feedback they receive" (Dowden et al. 350).

To address these issues, this text will introduce classroom-tested feedback methods for commentary to ease hindrances and increase engagement in the process for the greater satisfaction of everyone involved.

This text features curriculum and instruction to assist instructors in the humanities (English, history, philosophy, and so forth) in commenting on student drafts. To make a complex process more accessible, this text features strategies for both handwritten, auditory, and online commentary. To make the process more efficient, this text includes a variety of tools. To make the methods more relevant in many secondary and college writing-based courses, this text offers real strategies for applicability.

Although the sample papers are from college English and history courses as well as a college essay application, the methods are applicable in many other secondary and college writing-based courses. This text offers a fresh approach to feedback as a tool for continued teaching and learning.

Features of the text include:

- sample interrelated writing assignments, rubrics, and feedback models—all based on common rhetorical principles
- lists of available comments or "commenting vocabularies" (I wish I had had access to these as a new teacher)

- sample student papers reflecting (and not reflecting) traits of useful comments
- various models and templates for delivering audio and online commentary
- taxonomies/exercises to communicate about commentary
- strategies to manage students' emotional responses to feedback, using a more constructive tone and word choices for both greater impact across drafts and strengthening the trust factor inherent in their interactions
- strategies for "feed-forward" and self-regulation to raise students' rhetorical awareness of their own writing and provide feedback to inform instructors' teaching practices

The text focuses only on students' nonfiction (i.e., persuasive writing or arguments supported with credible sources, except for blog posts). One of the most effective approaches to commenting on persuasive writing is using rubrics: weight 75% for content (essay and paragraph levels) and 25% for conventions (style, format, and sentence level). These percentages mimic the SAT II (essay) model, which is familiar to many students.

For the purposes of this text, the scope is limited to handwritten, audio, and online commentary, though other useful platforms (videos, podcasts, and "live" chats) are becoming more widespread in the feedback process.

The text is filled with questions and answers for easier reference and user friendliness. Providing feedback leaves some instructors feeling despair after an arduous, time-consuming process when students may only respond with cursory glances at the comments or just throw the papers in the trash can. This text presents ways to enhance the feedback process by helping students see the benefits of comments on their writing.

This text also presents ways to reduce the amount of time instructors spend commenting as well as guidance for commentary with strategies for meaningful, impactful comments. Following this broad look at theory and process, the content will move to the granular level of *how* to deliver the amount and type of feedback that vary by instructors' purposes and assignments considering all aspects of the feedback process.

CHAPTER 1

The Feedback Process

"Feedback . . . fills a gap between what is understood and what is aimed to be understood . . . and it can lead to increased effort, motivation, or engagement to reduce the discrepancy between the current status and the goal."—John Hattie and Shirley Clarke, *Visible Learning Feedback*, 2–3

Note: For the purposes of this text, the terms "feedback" and "commentary/comments" are used interchangeably. These terms are guidelines on what is expected, and the extent to which students did or did not meet these expectations.

Feedback can serve as a motivator for students to improve their writing because feedback, both informal and formal (educational assessments and grades) as well as from jobs, sports, clubs, family, friends, and more, is always part of our students' lives. Without feedback, their development would be limited as it is difficult to assess themselves. This text supports approaches to students growing in self-assessment skills and learning, with meaningful feedback. In the act of feedback, trust means everything; without it, student writers may not self-actualize in the development process.

Instructors play a pivotal role in building trust, starting with a steady belief that students can improve as writers through different experiences in which they are allowed choices and view learning as a process. When these principles are in place, instructors find that their comments have greater impact on student writing.

What Are the Guiding Questions of This Text?

1. How can the feedback process become more effective for student-writing development and less burdensome for instructors in a time of large classes with numerous writing assignments?
2. How can instructors engage students more in the feedback process to achieve greater gains in their writing development?
3. How can instructors and students lessen the gap between their intentions and perceptions to have a greater impact on writing development?

What Are the Premises of This Text?

Drawing from classroom research, discussions with colleagues, and years of teaching composition at the high school and college levels, I have come to the conclusion that feedback

- is an essential part of student learning
- improves performance, changes behavior, and motivates or demotivates student writers
- is more effective with fewer meaningful, in-depth comments rather than a series of small corrections; "less is more"
- is most effective with consistency among assignments, rubrics, and commentary
- should promote engagement for students to become actively involved in self-reflection and self-regulation of their own learning during the writing process
- should allow for revision opportunities to apply in drafts during the writing process
- is related to writing as an iterative process in which student writers develop as they receive, comprehend, and act on feedback they receive after each writing assignment
- serves both formative and summative assessments
- has higher impact on revisions if papers are returned within ten days after submission so that feedback, like chewed gum, does not lose its flavor
- impacts revisions more productively if it focuses primarily on content and secondarily on sentence-level issues

- has greater impact using a rhetorical approach in which students learn to write responsively to primary audiences and purposes beyond the classroom
- is coupled with a strong examined emotional component: comments can trigger students' own beliefs about themselves as writers, positively or negatively
- is helpful if instructors seek "feedback on their feedback" to inform instruction

Instructors . . .

- tend to view feedback as more fair, constructive, encouraging, and useful than students do
- approach feedback as the students they were, often thorough and conscientious

Students . . .

- have untapped potential as writers
- bring the totality of their experiences with feedback to each new paper, especially at the beginning of new courses; they interpret feedback through the filter of the past
- tend to have a "short-termist" view of assignments
- learn more efficiently and effectively when they have a clear sense of how they're doing and what to improve
- need to be kept "teachable" and open to further learning, rather than turned off from the feedback process
- tend to view feedback in terms of grades; they do not always use feedback for learning but, rather, to compare/contrast their grades with classmates' and their previous papers
- revise in consistently narrow and predictable ways, unless guided otherwise; they tend to fear destruction and reconstruction of their drafts, especially if they have already invested adequate time in their writing

What Roles Do Instructors Play in Commentary Practices?

Instructors play the roles of appreciator, adviser, evaluator, assessor, gatekeeper, critiquer, ranker, redirector, editor, reviser, reader, judge, jury, listener, corrector, and decision maker, among others. With these roles, no wonder commenting on papers is draining. Instructors must shift from supportive editor and mentor to gatekeeper and assessor—and sometimes students find it hard to understand and appreciate the differences. They often want us to stay in only the softer, supportive roles, but to grow as writers they need to learn how to receive constructive criticism.

What Do Both Instructors and Students Want Regarding Feedback?
Instructors and students both want to be understood. They both want the other's attention paid to writing and comments. They both want improved writing. Students want explicit instructions on how to do better in revisions and future writing assignments, and instructors want application of their commentary in revision and future writing assignments.

What Are Instructors' Concerns About the Feedback Process?
Students . . .

- do not read comments beyond the first few and keep their focus mainly on grades
- have reading challenges with the assignment and comments
- lack self-awareness of their writing abilities and performance
- revise only on the surface level, not in structural/deeper ways

What Are Students' Concerns About the Feedback Process?
Instructors . . .

- do not always write legibly
- provide too many comments that are difficult to prioritize
- sometimes are too critical
- wait too long to return papers, and their comments seem irrelevant

What Are the General Principles of Feedback That This Text Advocates?

- gives attention to the rhetorical situation of the writing assignment
- appears clear and legible, if handwritten

- concentrates on the writing process rather than the product
- diagnoses larger issues rather than sentence-level issues (until the editing phase)
- explains how students can improve
- consists of a few well-developed comments rather than a series of shorter comments, applying the "less is more" principle
- focuses on writing productively rather than on student writers negatively
- stays relevant
- is suited to student writers
- is timely
- is useful

What Is the Theory or Framework of the Text?

First, this text assumes a developmental model in which feedback practices can help students understand how to improve and develop their writing by acquiring skills.

Second, with explicitness in mind, this text uses the framework of the rhetorical situation in Corbet and Connors's *Classic Rhetoric for the Modern Student* (figure 1.1). Most students will recognize this model from their AP language and composition courses. Students tend to find this visual useful to frame writing assignments.

Third, for the purposes of this text, "rhetoric" is defined as writers discovering what will work in given situations. Rhetoric involves persuasion that adapts to situations with given purposes for primary audiences.

Fourth, this text focuses on assigning primary (target) audiences beyond the classroom to build rhetorical awareness. Most students have never written for a variety of audiences beyond instructors and benefit from practice writing to "real" people to whom they may write in future careers. Primary audiences help students shape their writing through choices that respond to the rhetorical situation of the writing assignment (e.g., persuade a town council to fund road repairs in your hometown).

Fifth, this text's rhetorical approach (as exhibited in figure 1.1) is applicable to different disciplines in the humanities.

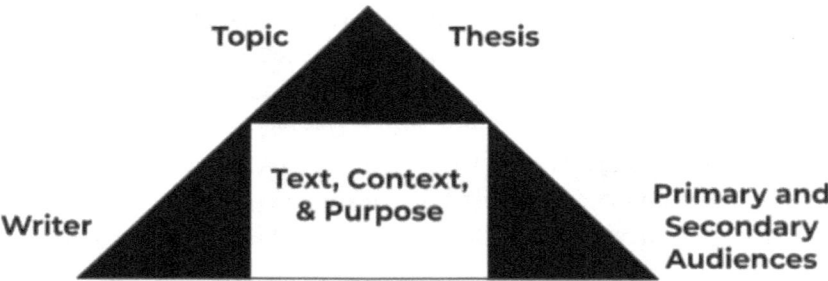

Figure 1.1. The Rhetorical Triangle. *Author created*

Writing assignments, rubrics, and commentary reflect elements of the rhetorical triangle:

- topic (subject)
- thesis (argument and position)
- writer (student as a developing academic writer)
- audience (primary: selected audience outside the classroom to whom students direct their writing; secondary: instructor who acts as an "audience of one"; and peers)
- text (paper, posting, speech)
- context (when and where submitted, posted, or delivered)
- purpose (reason for writing: explain, narrate, analyze, persuade)

What Are the Benefits and Roles Relative to Primary and Secondary Audiences?

In humanities courses, instructors can encourage students to select a relevant primary audience to persuade of their position. The audience reminds students that their writing is meant to be read and understood by "real" people. Examples include town councils, government officials, parent–teacher organizations, philosophical or psychological societies (e.g., historical organizations such as Daughters of the American Revolution), and others. The objective is for students to imagine how audiences may respond to each part of their argument.

Although students think of instructors as primary audiences who grade their writing and external audiences as "artificial," they can now think of instructors as secondary audience members who act in a unique role as an "audience of one" to "dramatize [the] presence of a reader" (Sommers xi). Their peers also serve as secondary audiences who, in turn, comment on whether writers' arguments persuade their primary audiences.

Why Is the Feedback and Learning Process Sometimes Labored, Even Burdensome?

Academic "writing is not a mother tongue" (Sommers, xii), which suggests that students' learning to write academically is a slow, yet deliberate process that requires steady, meaningful feedback for increased rhetorical awareness. Students try on academic voices (similar to trying on coats to see which one fits best) as they experiment and grow as writers across years of secondary and college instruction and practice.

Despite their backgrounds, they need opportunities to practice code switching from informal to formal expression. They need to try on different voices until their own emerges—as they become more comfortable writing academically until it becomes more of a "mother tongue." They need room to make mistakes with, for example, mixing voices—sometimes sounding like an adolescent; at other times, sounding like a professional—and receive constructive advice to be more consistent.

To expect fast progress is unrealistic as these processes are recursive and nonlinear. To expect reasonable progress—even one step forward, two steps back—is a fair-minded way to approach the feedback and learning processes. It takes patience with students, as it may take years to master academic writing as a "mother tongue."

What common words do instructors use to describe their time (and frustration) spent on the feedback process?

- constant
- extensive
- frustrating
- insufficient
- tedious
- time consuming

Figure 1.2. The Instructors' Comic Strip. *Created by Jonny Jimison*

How Does the Feedback Process Relate to the Kübler-Ross Model of Grief Stages?

> Denial: If I don't think about the papers, I don't have to grade them, right? I'll clean my car, home, even the garage before I grade papers.
> Anger: Why do I have to spend my weekend grading papers? Why don't I have a job without my own "homework"? What did they learn from my instruction about writing assignments? Why don't they address my comments from the last paper?
> Bargaining: I enjoy teaching English, but some days I wish I taught algebra. Well, they did address some comments, but not all; they reflect half of the skills that I taught, but not 100%. If I teach the element (e.g., introducing quotes, paraphrasing) again, these problems in students' papers will diminish.
> Depression: I'm grading paper number 44 with 26 more to go. Why didn't my students make more progress since we workshopped all major parts of the papers? I thought my instruction was more effective and impactful.
> Acceptance: Learning is incremental, step-by-step, sometimes sideways, backward, and forward; writing is a slow, complex process that takes frequent reinforcement. Everyone needs an editor. I'll keep trying and reframing how I teach writing assignments and comment on papers while keeping my sanity.

How Can the Feedback Process Become More Manageable?

Even though English instructors' comments may imply that students apply them in subsequent drafts, students tend to compartmentalize writing assignments, not view them as interconnected. This is particularly true if instructors use summative comments on "final" drafts, which, in this holistic approach, students typically read only for major comments and grade justifications. If instructors comment formatively on drafts *during* the writing process, students are more likely to address them in revisions, particularly if instructors have conveyed their inherent value.

What Is Key About Alignment of All Parts of the Writing/Feedback Processes?

The key is aligning language of classroom, writing assignments, rubrics, and commentary; content and conventions.

How Do Instructors Know How Much Commentary to Provide?

The amount depends on the instructor's assignment and purpose. More feedback does not always equal more learning or writing development. Fewer, more meaningful comments rather than a series of short responses about sentence-level issues typically have more impact.

How Frequently Should an Instructor Comment on Drafts?

If it's part of a writing process as opposed to an in-class essay exam, the focus should be more on formative assessment (within the writing process), rather than a summative assessment (at the end of the writing process). By providing feedback on rough drafts, students have opportunities to apply instructors' comments. Students can then provide "feedback on feedback" on instructors' commentary to report misperceptions so that instructors can clarify before students finish final drafts. With a large course load, if it is not realistic to provide feedback until the final drafts, students could still have the opportunity to address comments in the next writing assignment, but it's best done deliberately with a "feedback on feedback" exercise.

Which Forms of Commentary Are Useful and Current, and How Are Digital Tools and Models Helpful in the Feedback Process?

In the digital age, functions of written, audio, and video commentary through *Desire to Learn* (D2L), *Blackboard*, and other systems are accessible and economical options for instructors. These functions support (1) commenting on different assessments, (2) tailoring to individual students, and (3) soliciting students' perceptions of the commentary. Because writing for audiences is a social act or conversation, using digital comments (audio and online) engages students and instructors in a conversation about feedback.

For years, the author has used D2L to audiotape comments to which students listen—often several times—then tape their own comments back to communicate (or miscommunicate) their perceptions, which has proved enlightening. With consistent use of audio commentary, students' degree of comfort and understanding is higher, and the transfer to subsequent papers is more likely. Doing audio comments is an easier method of conveying meaning.

What Approaches Ensure That the Feedback Process Is Fair and Equitable?

- Be mindful of (+/−) biases that inform our responses: impatience, intolerance, favoritism, affirmation, and so forth.
- Focus on the writing process rather than student writers and their motives.
- Have grade-norming sessions.
- Respond to blind copies of students' writing; it should not include identifying information, and drafts should have only numbers instead of names.
- Reverse/resequence the order of students' papers for subsequent assignments; mix up the order of papers when commenting. We can become stuck in the "anger" or "depression" stages when commenting, especially closer to the bottom of the stack, and tend to be tougher on students in that group than students in the earlier group. For the next round, start with student papers from the latter group.
- Review by supervisors of one or two student papers or reports from each instructor to ensure consistency.

What Feedback Strategies Improve Student Writing Development (as discussed in this text)?

- Ask students to write reflections on how they plan to address feedback.
- Comment on one or two paragraphs and ask students to apply feedback.
- Devote class time to explaining assignments and the feedback philosophy/method.
- Incorporate 1:1 draft conferences into the writing process.
- Show model papers.

- Stay loyal to rubrics.
- Use handouts for conventions: citations and sentence-level issues.
- Use track changes for comments.

What Questions Should Instructors Ask Themselves About Their Feedback Early and Later in the Writing Process?

1. What is my feedback trying to convey and achieve?
2. How do students experience my feedback? Constructive? Destructive? Somewhere in between?
3. How does my feedback ensure that students know how their current performance measures up to good/expected performance (as conveyed in class, rubrics, and other ways)?
4. How does my feedback foster students' self-assessment skills?
5. Should I provide opportunities for revision? If so, when?

The following chapters will help instructors answer these questions to best serve students' writing development.

CHAPTER 2

Writing Assignments

"Academic writing is not a mother tongue; its conventions require instruction and practice, years of imitation, and experimentation in rehearsing other people's arguments before being able to articulate our own."—Sommers, *Responding to Student Writers*, xii

This chapter takes a look at writing assignments as they relate to the writing-process cycle, feedback, assessments, and rubrics, which will be covered in the next several chapters. Many valuable books on construction of all parts of writing assignments are on the market for further reference.

To start, how do writing assignments relate to academic writing that is not a "mother tongue"? Because writing assignments offer opportunities to instruct students on parts of the writing process such as content and conventions, they offer more practice with academic language as it becomes increasingly familiar to them.

What Are the Fundamental Objectives of Writing Assignments?

The four fundamental objectives of writing assignments are to

1. gain opportunity to learn
2. extend knowledge
3. understand writing as a process
4. raise awareness about primary audiences: perhaps altering their beliefs and perspectives—and helping them to discover new ways of thinking about topics

Designing a good writing assignment supports careful commenting practices. If an assignment is too vague or too difficult to understand, comments may fail to reach students.

What Is at Issue With Objectives of Writing Assignments?

None of the objectives can be achieved if instructors waste too much time commenting on papers (e.g., explaining the unexplained or minimalistic writing assignment, instead of looking at the quality of students' writing).

What Are Examples of Objectives?

- analyze evidence
- read sources critically
- practice persuasive writing
- use proper citations
- respond to a rhetorical situation (what are important features of writing assignments?)
- align with rubric
- use careful wording (e.g., carefully summarize in an articulately, clear, and concise manner)
- make structure and organization consistent with other writing assignments in the course
- use conventions (for purposes of this text, "conventions" are defined as surface features: title, grammar, punctuation, diction, transitions, MLA or another style for citations and works cited/consulted). Clarify which conventions are required for each assignment.
- set forth the criteria (it may be on the rubric)
- convey deadlines for draft(s)
- explain how the assignment will be graded and when/how feedback will be provided
- set the format (structure and organization of the paper)
- state the objectives clearly (e.g., research skills)
- make a paper readable
- describe the rhetorical situation surrounding assignment
- use the same vocabulary in class lectures and discussions about writing in the assignment

What Is Important to Avoid When Constructing Writing Assignments?
Anything that is too

- casual
- dense
- dependent on students' background knowledge, requiring them to "read between the lines" (i.e., supply too much of their own meaning, which may or may not align with assignment objectives)
- general
- high-level vocabulary (e.g., "exigency"), unless defined in class or in the assignment
- inconsistent with other writing assignments
- lengthy
- lacking in key features (see the aforementioned list)

Why Is It Important to Emphasize the Concept of "Audience" in Writing Assignments?
When students write for a "real" audience outside the classroom, they tend to raise the level of responsiveness of their writing. Their writing seems more awakened, which is important because the overarching writing goal is for students to learn to manage how they want writing to be read and how to persuade audiences through their arguments. Raising students' rhetorical awareness of their writing by making better choices about words, ideas, arrangement, and emphasis is the way to ensure responsiveness to the rhetorical situations surrounding writing assignments.

What Is a Common Way in Which High School and First-Year College Students Conceptualize Audience?
Often, they assume instructors are the only audiences; therefore, they have no need to explain information that she already knows. (This is a particular problem with essay exams.) Likewise, students tend to think of audience by proximity: their instructors are present and will grade assignments; therefore, they have no need to write for external audiences. To the contrary, instructors need to discuss the benefits of writing to primary audiences for practice in future writing in the "real world."

What Is a Pedagogical Approach to Writing for Audiences?

One is writing an audience analysis, a paragraph that answers these questions: Who? Gender? Race? Ethnicity? Age Range? Socioeconomic Class? Age Range? Educational Level? Investment in Topic? Level of Agreement/Disagreement with Thesis? And/or Geographic Location? Analyzing a primary audience can help students answer these questions: What do you want the audience to feel and learn? What do you want to persuade them of?

If students are having trouble conceptualizing primary audiences, what are useful approaches to assist them?

- First, write the assignment as a letter to their primary audiences. This will encourage students to consider the audience and increase the responsiveness of their writing to the rhetorical situation of the assignment.
- Second, think about where writing may appear for its audience: website, journal, newspaper, pamphlet, or other. Of course, students must consider the values of the primary audiences to write responsively to them.
- Third, have them write an audience analysis paragraph in which they identify the primary audience, its characteristics (e.g., race, gender, age range, educational level, geographical location, and more) and level of agreement or disagreement with the student's position in his or her thesis statement.
- And, fourth, hold a discussion about how primary audiences in academia differ from those on social media platforms such as Twitter and Facebook.

What Is a Suggested Approach to Introducing Writing Assignments (and More) to Students?

Discuss the writing assignment: the rhetorical situation, including the purpose, audience, objectives, and guidelines. Then ask students to articulate the objectives and guidelines to ensure understanding; the rubrics—purpose, criterion, and scales (see chapter 4 for further explanation of rubrics); your approach to commenting on papers; and the Invention Worksheet (see below for both form and sample).

How Is an Invention Worksheet Beneficial for Raising Students' Rhetorical Awareness?

Students plan their writing by thinking through the rhetorical situation and the choices they will make for their primary audiences. The worksheet allows for active inquiry and revisions before and during the writing process. Further, the worksheet reduces anxiety about the writing assignment as it helps students start building knowledge and making beneficial decisions (see the sample Invention Worksheet below).

SAMPLE INVENTION WORKSHEET FOR RESEARCH PROPOSAL, WRITING ASSIGNMENT #1

The following is a helpful prewriting exercise for students to plan their research proposal.

Prompts: What is the central problem? What is a proposed solution? What are the benefits of the solution?
Text (What is the format of the proposal?)
Context (Where?) Where does the problem occur in your hometown, state, or country (the last one, for international students)?
Purpose (Why?)
General Problem (What?)
Narrowed Problem (Ways to narrow: age range, time frame, one type or aspect of problem, gender, religion, socioeconomic class, profession/job, geographical area, etc.)
Solution (How? Examine the existing one or propose one—with evidence.)
Benefits of the Solution for the Primary Audience (What? For whom?)
Audience: Primary (Who is directly invested in the problem? Who will implement the solution? Who will benefit from the solution?)
Audience: Secondary (Who is indirectly invested in the problem? Who will implement the solution? Who will benefit from the solution?)
Rhetorical Appeal (ethos, pathos, logos): Primary—Which one will govern your proposal?
Rhetorical Appeal (ethos, pathos, logos): Secondary—Which one will guide your proposal in a more minor way?

Guiding Question: Open-ended question beginning with "How?" or "Why?" (Your thesis—and proposal—will answer this question.)
Narrowed Guiding Question
Preliminary or Working Thesis (needs to identify the problem, solution, and benefits)
Refined Thesis

Sources to support proposal:

- scholarly article (peer-reviewed)
- news article (reviewed and selected by editors)
- website
- book (hard copy or e-copy)
- interview
- other

SAMPLE WRITING ASSIGNMENT #1: RESEARCH PROPOSAL

Assignment Overview: Research writing is formal and scholarly. Writers develop viewpoints on topics and gather credible research to support their positions. Using explanations to "reveal" their answers to proposed research questions, writers need to guard against mere summaries of facts, which produce dispassionate words that do not show evidence of critical thinking.

As a writer, your challenge is to choose an interesting topic, locate sources, take clear and accurate notes, develop a perspective on your topic, and write a research paper that shows the angle that you take on the subject. Further, your analysis is crucial; make every effort to explain the significance of your assertions (e.g., explain Why? or How?). Make every effort to cite your sources. Make every effort to use your own "voice" in your writing. Challenge yourself to make assertions and cite sources, not make others' assertions and cite yourself.

Research writing is, in itself, persuasive, because a burden rests on you to argue that your topic has value and interest, not to mention integrity. Use means of persuasion (i.e., statistics, facts, examples, appeals to logic/emotion/ethics, and others) to support your position.

It is important to choose a position, point of view, or stance to support your paper.

The final paper requires you to collect your knowledge about writing well-conceived papers and demonstrate your understanding of what it means to write for readers—those whose investment (in your topic), biases, gender, race, and educational status shape their viewpoint. In other words, you need to choose an audience and direct your writing to them. As you write about an arguable topic, consider what words "do" in relation to your identified readers: empower? defeat? generate emotions? convince? deter? Keep them in mind all through your writing.

First, generate three questions about your topic. Second, narrow to one overriding question that focuses the entire content of your research paper. Third, allow some thinking time to determine the central question that your paper will answer.

Background: As Maimon, Peritz, and Yancey state in *A Writer's Resource*, proposals "are designed to cause change [of an issue]" (126). As a future leader in business, law, education, or other, people will look to you to propose changes to decision makers. Undoubtedly, you will write many proposals, because you are expected to act as a leader with a vision to improve situations and processes. In other words, the onus rests on you to notice problems, make "reasoned assertion[s]" about them, and propose solutions—to become and remain solution-oriented (Maimon, Peritz, and Yancey 126).

Assignment: Locate a social justice problem in your hometown, city, or state. It can exist at a local, national, or global level. The problem may relate to the following: food, education, health, politics, science, infrastructure, children, adolescents, the elderly, race, gender, or another topic. The main point is that your topic must have a human element (in other words, how does the problem affect people?).

Prompt: What is a significant problem related to a social justice issue in your home state? What is a potential solution to the problem? What are the benefits of the solution?

Sample Problem: The lack of visibility/rights of indigenous populations in northern Alaska. Solution: Increased frequency and quantity of indigenous population's coverage by mainstream media. Benefits: Raised cultural awareness of contributions of indigenous populations.

Topic: Needs to meet the following criteria:

- allows for an interview with an expert or key stakeholder
- is focused and narrowed to a major problem and solution, with multiple benefits
- is a real problem that currently exists
- yields credible, scholarly research

Text: A proposal is different from a standard research paper in these ways: it includes headings and subheadings; it has a specific, "real" primary audience; and it advocates for a specific problem, solution, and benefits for the audience.

Primary Audience: Educated adult decision maker(s) who is/are in position to implement solution(s).

Content:

- Sources: Consult and cite a minimum of five credible primary sources in your research proposal. These five sources must include at least three scholarly articles (or two articles and one book), one credible website (e.g., newspaper), and one interview. You can add secondary sources.
- Interview: Identify an expert and/or key stakeholder, develop interview questions, and conduct an interview as a part of your proposal #4 research process. You are required to receive approval from your instructor regarding the intended interviewee/subject, mode of communication with the subject, and interview questions before establishing communication for the interview. Start this process early. Be sure to include the interviewee's transcribed responses in your final proposal #4 submission package. Do not identify parents or siblings as interviewees; your audience wants to see evidence of your effort to locate an expert on the problem/solution and engage in field research.

Conventions:

- Documentation: Use MLA style to cite quotes/paraphrases and for works cited/works consulted.
- Editing: Proofread for spelling, punctuation, and grammatical errors so as not to distract your primary audience and keep your ethos.

- Format (structure and organization):
  - Provide a title that links to the thesis—in your own words.
  - Include an introductory, body, and concluding paragraphs; an arguable thesis toward the end of the introductory paragraph; and cited quotes/paraphrases (rule of thumb is 2–3 per page).
- Style:
  - Diction: academic; avoid casual language (it, thing, ended up, a lot, etc.)
  - Syntax: clear, edited sentences
  - Tone: academic, appropriate for primary audience
  - Point of View: third person
- Length: 1,300–1,500 words

SAMPLE WRITING ASSIGNMENT #2: RHETORICAL ANALYSIS

Assignment: Analyze a newspaper article rhetorically. Examine all parts of the rhetorical situation surrounding the article: primary audience (main audience to whom the article is directed), purpose, message (thesis), and context (when and where published).

Prompts: What is the author's central argument? How does the author support his or her argument?

Text: Choose one article from the newspaper.

Primary Audience: Educated adults who have read the article but have not analyzed it deeply

Content:

Choose one of the following articles to analyze:

- "Is a Jogging Ban in Sierra Leone for Safety or to Suppress Opposition?" by Jaime Yaya Barry (*New York Times*) https://www.nytimes.com/2017/08/27/world/africa/sierra-leone-freetown-jogging-ban.html
- "For Afghan Girls' Robotics Team, U.S. Visa Denial Was Last of Many Hurdles" by Pamela Constable (*Washington Post*) https://www.washingtonpost.com/world/asia_pacific/for-afghan-girls-robotics-team-us-visa-denial-was-last-of-many-hur

dles/2017/07/07/f4afd606-6035-11e7-80a2-8c226031ac3f_story.html?utm_term=.fba6b03cf380
- "Syrian Dancer Flying, Looking for Freedom (Landing in Amsterdam)" by Nina Siegal (*New York Times*) https://www.nytimes.com/2017/08/25/arts/dance/syrian-dancer-ahmad-joudeh-amsterdam-dutch-national-ballet.html?rref=collection%2Fsectioncollection%2Feurope&action=click&contentCollection=europe&region=stream&module=stream_unit&version=latest&contentPlacement=23&pgtype=sectionfront

Conventions:

- Documentation: Use MLA style to cite quotes/paraphrases and for works cited/works consulted.
- Editing: Proofread for spelling, punctuation, and grammatical errors so as to not distract your primary audience and keep your ethos.
- Format (Structure and Organization):
    - Provide a title that links to thesis—in your own words.
    - Include an introductory, body, and concluding paragraphs; an arguable thesis toward the end of the introductory paragraph; and cited quotes/paraphrases (rule of thumb is 2–3 per page).
- Style
    - Diction: Academic; avoid casual language (it, thing, ended up, a lot, etc.)
    - Syntax: Clear, edited sentences
    - Tone: Academic, appropriate for a primary audience
    - Point of View: third person
- Length: 800–1,000 words

SAMPLE WRITING ASSIGNMENT #3: SHORT REFLECTION ON COURSE TOPIC

Assignment: Reflecting upon our discussions about gender, write a short reflection paper on one prompt.

Prompts:

- What is the state of feminism today? What have you observed and/or participated in that suggests where feminism lies in this "Fourth Wave: 2008–Present"?

Or

- What are stereotypes of men and/or women? Why are stereotypes true or untrue? What have you observed or participated in that supports your position?

Text: In-class paper written under time constraints
Primary Audience: Educated adults who have some knowledge of your topic but will learn more from your argument and experiences.
Content: Use notes, documents, PowerPoint slides, terms lists, and/or other course texts.
Conventions:

- Documentation: Use MLA style to cite quotes/paraphrases and for works cited/works consulted.
- Editing: Proofread for spelling, punctuation, and grammatical errors so as to not distract your primary audience and keep your ethos.
- Format (Structure and Organization):
  - Provide a title that links to thesis—in your own words.
  - Include an introductory, body, and concluding paragraphs; an arguable thesis toward the end of the introductory paragraph; and cited quotes/paraphrases (rule of thumb is 2–3 per page).
- Style:
  - Diction: Academic; avoid casual language (it, thing, ended up, a lot, etc.)
  - Syntax: Clear, edited sentences
  - Tone: Academic, appropriate for a primary audience
  - Point of View: first person
- Length: Minimum of 450 words; maximum is decided given time allotted.

CHAPTER 3

Assessment

> "Assessment is an integral part of instruction, as it determines whether or not the goals of education are being met. Assessment inspires us to ask these hard questions: 'Are we teaching what we think we are teaching?' 'Are students learning what they are supposed to be learning?' 'Is there a way to teach the subject better, thereby promoting better learning?'"—Edutopia.org

Learning: As educators, we are constantly examining it, looking for it, assessing it, and reexamining it. We assess learning informally (i.e., observation such as "Juanita seems detached today . . . will check in with her after class") and formally (i.e., exams and writing assignments). We look for subtle and not-so-subtle evidence or proof of students' understanding or misunderstanding of our lessons.

Assessments are a powerful teaching tool that assists instructors in gauging students' learning and serve as a key component of the feedback process.

Assessment helps to answer those "hard questions" to look both ways: outward toward students and inward for the instructors. In the past, the focus has been on evaluating products of students' work, but assessment—as is more common in the past decade—focuses on the process and helps students improve their learning and instructors improve their teaching effectiveness.

DEFINITIONS OF "EVALUATION" AND "ASSESSMENT"

What Is Assessment?

Assessment is an active process during the learning cycle to determine the extent to which students learn concepts. The process first establishes criteria, then uses criteria to assess learning. Assessment is always dependent on context, which means that instructors' assignments and purpose of commenting styles need consideration.

Difference Between Assessment and Evaluation

Assessment is feedback or appraisal of students' work during or at the end of a learning process—for example, an instructor's feedback on rough drafts about Lieutenant Ted Lavender's controversial role in Tim O'Brien's *The Things They Carried*. On the other hand, *evaluation* is a professional judgment call about the quality and performance of students' work or "products"—for instance, an instructor's grades on a group project about Shakespeare's comedies.

In summary, *assessment* focuses on process, identification of strengths and needs, and descriptive feedback, whereas *evaluation* focuses on products, judgment on the basis of criteria, and numerical scores. *Assessment* takes place *as* learning happens, and *evaluation* takes place *after* learning happens.

Difference Between Formative and Summative Assessments

Formative assessment takes place during a learning process, yields insights for both instructors and students, and influences learning. *Summative* assessment takes place at the conclusion of a learning process, "sums up" overall student performance, and justifies grades. For example, a formative assessment is the doctor's monitoring of patients' negative or positive responses to treatment, whereas a summative assessment is a doctor's diagnosis with prescribed medicine or other treatment.

What Does Formative Assessment "Look Like" in the Classroom?

- instructors using feedback to expand and accelerate learning
- students taking a more proactive role to interpret feedback (i.e., continually monitor their own motivation, thinking, and behavior during learning processes)
- instructors incorporating data from feedback and students' responses to feedback into the curriculum (e.g., future writing assignments) and instruction of unclear concepts in previous feedback (e.g., "paraphrase more accurately," which students may have misunderstood how to address), leading to stronger writing development

What Are the Hallmarks of Effective Formative Assessments?

- clear objectives
- understandable, relevant feedback
- opportunities to act on feedback
- informing teaching

INFORMAL AND FORMAL ASSESSMENTS

What Are Examples of Informal and Formal Assessments?

Informal

- observations in the classroom
- surveys
- questioning
- checklists
- think-pair-share

Formal

- exams
- final projects and portfolios
- lab reports
- graded discussions

How Is Commentary Related to Assessment?
Learning = formative; commentary = assessment.

FUNCTIONS AND QUALITIES OF EFFECTIVE AND INEFFECTIVE COMMENTS

What Is at Issue with Ineffective Comments?

Though instructors may write cryptic, sarcastic, and fastidious comments, especially when grading paper number 47 in a pile of 75, this can easily devolve into an exercise in futility that fails to reinforce desired writing behavior. Pitiless comments can profoundly affect students' confidence as writers; they tend to assume that these comments, which are often ineffective, reveal that their instructors "liked or disliked" their writing, or even them as writers.

Damage from tough comments is sometimes substantial; these comments are classified as "thunderstruck" (i.e., ones that feel similar to "stings" not easily forgotten). For example, "I expected more of you. You'll never be a strong writer."

These comments limit writing development and bring resentment. Instead, this text calls for guidance of students as thinkers who can read and write in increasingly critical ways. Feedback should open up, not shut down the learning process; it should assess, not oppress students.

Ineffective comments do not tell students that they have untapped potential as writers. To reach that potential, instructors can show students *how* to improve their writing through mutual engagement in the feedback process that also involves students learning to accept and benefit from feedback, to see it as constructive rather than disparaging.

Functions of Ineffective and Effective Assessment Criteria for Writing Assignments

Ineffective

- Enacts too many purposes: descriptive, analytical, evaluation, leaving students confused as to the primary purpose
- Focuses too heavily on sentence-level correctness, even though the grammar section of a rubric is assigned fewer points, which is contradictory

- Includes criteria that point to expectation of perfection rather than excellence

Effective

- Is used to improve the quality of students' work
- Explains all parts of the writing assignment in greater depth
- Invites students to reexamine their thinking and expression
- Conveys values of courses
- Focuses on process and writing within it, rather than writers and their motives
- Supplies students with opportunities to apply feedback in drafts
- Places more emphasis on content (75%), less emphasis on conventions (25%)

Qualities of Ineffective and Effective Assessment Criteria for Writing Assignments

Ineffective (too directive or controlling)

- Becomes hyper-focused on sentence-level issues
- Contains dismissive or harsh words and tone
- Corrects only proofreading errors rather than content
- Delivers in academic language students may not understand
- Focuses on assumptions rather than facts and data
- Focuses on student personally rather than his or her argument
- Presents as too ambitious
- Takes ownership away from students; less encouragement of self-assessment
- Uses negative tones that are destructive and punitive

Effective (more facilitative)

- Is anchored near problematic areas
- Contains a mix of directive and facilitative comments
- Describes the discrepancy between the limitation/error and expected learning objectives

- Encourages transfer to revision opportunities and/or subsequent writing assignments
- Focuses mainly on 3–4 global issues in a prioritized way
- Is mindful of the rhetorical situation surrounding the assignment
- Is specific rather than general
- Responds as an "audience of one"
- Uses language that encourages active learning and self-assessment for students to "own" their writing; treats students as thinkers
- Uses the right amount (not too much, not too little) at the appropriate level where students learn best; "less is more"

What Are Examples of Ineffective Comments?

- ambiguous
- be more analytical
- be more collaborative
- be more proactive
- be specific
- edit
- elaborate
- fix
- rethink
- revise
- style should be more academic
- too brief
- you're a poor/lazy writer
- you will never become a strong writer
- vague
- work harder
- work on editing

DIRECTIVE VERSUS FACILITATIVE COMMENTS

What Are Examples of Controlling (Directive) and Noncontrolling (Facilitative) Comments?

Directive Comments

- Rewrite concluding sentence.
- Add ___, ___, and ___ to the thesis.
- Delete this paragraph.

Facilitative Comments

- What are you thinking here about this concluding sentence?
- What would the audience think should be added to the thesis? or Would the thesis, as stated, be persuasive to your primary audience?
- What are you trying to accomplish with this paragraph? Would your primary audience want to read this paragraph? Would this paragraph help to persuade your primary audience?

SAMPLE DRAFTS WITH TRACK CHANGES: FORMATIVE ASSESSMENT ON ROUGH DRAFT AND SUMMATIVE ASSESSMENT ON FINAL DRAFT

Note: An example of overbearing, directive comments.

Sample Paper with Ineffective Written Comments That Focus Only on Conventions

Ahulani's Research Paper Rough Draft (introduction and body paragraph)

Who? Freshman college student, Ahulani
What? Research proposal on topic related to home state
Where? English composition at a small college in New England
Prompt: What is a significant problem related to a social justice issue in your home state? What is a potential solution to the problem? What are the benefits of the solution?

Controversy Atop Mauna Kea

Ua mau ke ea o ka ʻāina i ka pono, "The life of the land is preserved in righteousness [KW1]." This phrase, originally stated by King Kamehameha III in a public address to his people in 1843, has become the State of Hawaii's motto [KW2] and it describes the mindset of many native Hawaiians (Kopper and Kalama).

As David Kalama and Camile Kopper explain, the state motto means [KW3] "It is sovereignty for our ʻāina, which includes land, people, and the reciprocal relationships between them that in turn gives us life, liberty, and true happiness" (Kalama and Kopper [KW4]).

This fundamental idea sets the stage for the larger heated debate over the construction of the Thirty Meter Telescope (TMT) on Mauna Kea today. According to the TMT Project website [KW5] the telescope will be built on 525 acres costing an estimated 1.4 billion dollars [KW6] to construct. However, building the Thirty Meter Telescope will boost the state of Hawaii into the forefront of science and astronomy.

In addition to the ancestral relationship [KW7] Native Hawaiians have with Mauna Kea Native Hawaiians are worried about the destruction of Mauna Kea which could impact the natural resources it had provided them for years. Mauna Kea currently has an aquifer which supplements the Big Island with fresh water (Final Environmental Impact Statement).

In ancient times, Native Hawaiians recognized this, that Mauna Kea was the source of life, feeding the plants and making life possible. Mauna Kea provided adze stone which was formed from the rapid cooling of lava from the ice on Mauna Kea [KW8].

[KW1: Put period inside quotes!]

[KW2: Need comma! Remember our review in class.]

[KW3: Add a colon.]

[KW4: Don't use names of authors twice in a given sentence.]

[KW5: Another comma problem. You need to address this distracting error!]

[KW6: Cite numbers and statistics. They are not paraphrasable.]

[KW7: Yet another comma error. Sigh!]

[KW8: Are these your words? Seems too academic. This could be plagiarism.]

The rapid cooling created dense, sturdy stone. A specialized group of Native Hawaiians quarried the stone and made Koi (adze) which was a prized tool used in ceremonies, crafting canoes, and many other necessary objects. As stated by a Native Hawaiian, it was "the most important tool" (A Temple Under Siege **[KW9]**). Mauna Kea has served as a cultural connection to deities, sacred land, and a resource of life for Hawaiians in ancient times and today.

[KW9: Punctuate title correctly.]

What is at issue with these written comments? Students will disengage from the writing process if comments focus only on conventions, especially those with an intolerant tone. They begin to see the instructor, not themselves, as owning the writing. In the rough draft stage, it is paramount to offer commentary on content, saving the editorial comments for the final drafting stage with a "less is more" approach.

Select 3–4 errors so students can educate themselves on grammar, punctuation, and usage rules and correct errors themselves. Of course, instructors have to comment on potential plagiarism, but using a more professional tone will engage students in avoiding trouble ahead.

So, how do instructors strike a balance between types of comments? The balance can come from directive and facilitative or reader-response comments. Both encourage instructors and students to engage in the feedback process together.

Instructors acting as readers or "audience of one" ensures that students focus on how primary audiences read and experience their writing. If instructors use only directive comments, students do not assume ownership of their writing, which is problematic for their growth as writers. However, instructors' facilitative commentary promotes student ownership of their writing.

Examples of a Balance of Directive and Facilitative Commentary

Directive

- I want you to add more citations.
- Your point about child-labor laws is not as persuasive as needed for audience.

- Your argument is circular, and it is hard to determine where it begins and ends.

Facilitative

- Think about adding _____.
- Adding examples here would lessen confusion and support your thesis.
- You've defined the term "consent" clearly and summarized the author's argument about the term. How can you tie both together? or What is your next step?

How Does Assessment Help Students to Develop as Writers?

Primarily, assessment serves to clarify issues, set goals, raise audience awareness, as persuasive writing always has a purpose to influence viewpoints of others, and, in turn, assess their abilities and progress more accurately.

IDEAL AND COMMON CYCLES OF WRITING AND FEEDBACK PROCESSES

What Are the Differences Between Ideal and Common Feedback Cycles of the Writing Process?

The ideal version features the best options to incorporate both formative and summative assessments; however, the common version features the typical process in which formative assessments are neglected in favor of only summative assessments, which leads to students addressing fewer comments on subsequent drafts. (An essay exam version would only call for summative assessments.)

The ideal version, which this text focuses on, has greater impact of instructors' commentary across drafts with both formative and summative assessments.

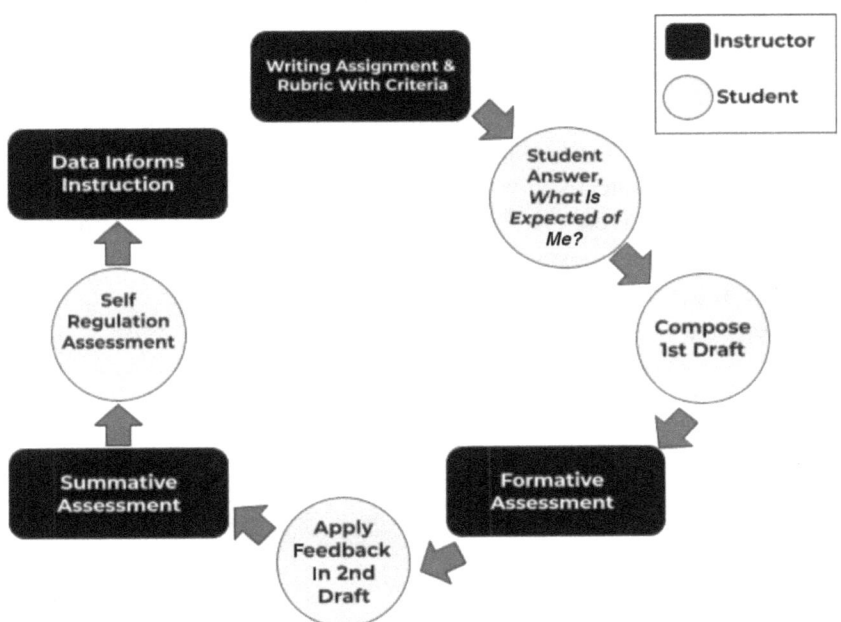

Figure 3.1. The Ideal Feedback Cycle of the Writing Process. *Author created*

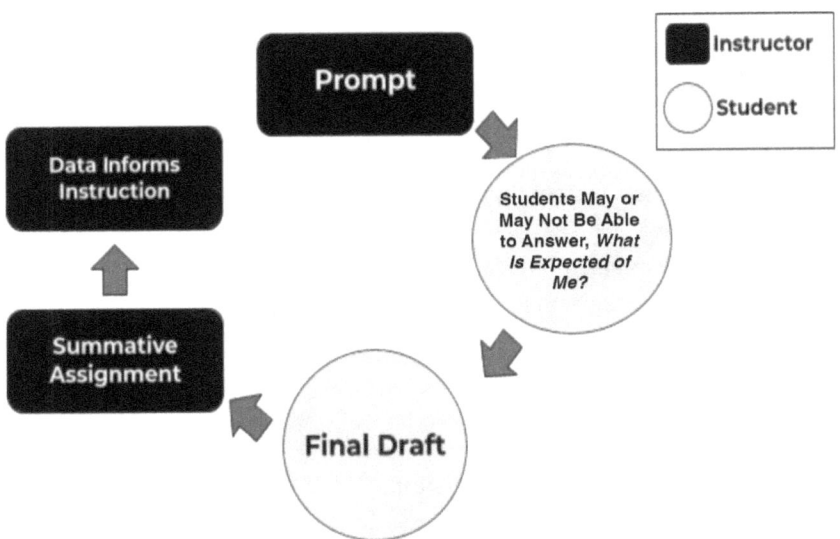

Figure 3.2. The Common Feedback Cycle of the Writing Process. *Author created*

How Can Instructors Discover Types of Feedback That Students Have Received from Past Instructors?

On the first day of class, issue a "Past Feedback Strengths and Needs for Writing" survey with an open-ended question: "Recalling your instructors' feedback on papers last year/semester in courses, what are your strengths and needs in writing academic papers?"

When I have given this survey in my first-year college English courses, general responses include the following (in alphabetical order). The most common responses (noted with *) appear on surveys every semester.

Writing Strengths

- explanations to support ideas
- flow
- formatting*
- ideas/creative thinking
- paragraph structure
- producing good evidence for thesis*
- putting ideas in sequential order/logical progression
- relevant points
- transitions*

Writing Needs

- coherent thesis statements*
- conciseness*
- detailing responses
- developing paragraphs
- editing
- expand vocabulary*
- flow*
- grammar and punctuation*
- keep content relevant to thesis/topic*
- knowing which main points to use for papers*
- more persuasive power
- organizing evidence

- reducing repetitiveness*
- revising
- spelling
- sustaining review and editing over lengthy process

The "strengths" list is always shorter than the "needs" list. Students tend to be tough on themselves, which is often a result of highly critical comments they have received in past classes.

Survey results should inform instruction, goal setting, and assessment. Returning to survey results mid-semester (or mid-year) with a discussion about progress and ways to adjust goals can prove valuable for the feedback process.

FORMATIVE AND SUMMATIVE ASSESSMENTS

The following are examples of formative and summative assessments.

Formative Assessment (During the Writing Process)

Here are three major areas of improvement for your rough draft:

1. Thesis is quite ambitious, covers many subtopics—a helpful approach to streamline your argument by asking yourself: Which 1–2 subtopics most effectively support my purpose and primary audience?
2. Evidence is imbalanced with analysis; there is much more evidence about _____ than your voice (thinking about evidence). Also, quotes are tossed in with the assumption that your audience will understand, but they may not. Quote sandwiches: introduction, quote, and analysis tied to topic sentence, and ultimately tied to thesis—are supportive to take charge of the persuasive power in your argument.
3. Conclusion needs more of your attention. What are your main points to summarize? synthesis about main points? strong finishing statement?

4. Keep working hard. Your argument has good potential, but remember to imagine how the audience will respond to each part. See me if you want to discuss further.

Summative Assessment

Rhetorical Analysis of an Argument

Background Information

- Rubric with Criteria Using Rhetorical Language
- English Composition Course
- Grade: 75% Content; 25% Conventions

*Highlighted areas need attention/revision

What are three areas of strength?
What are three areas in need of improvement?

Table 3.1. Sample Rubric with Performance Scales

Content (75%)	Excellent	Above Average	Average	Below Average	Poor or Absent
Introduction: Hook; title of article/author; author's credentials; transfer to thesis	all parts present and clear	most parts present and clear	some parts present and clear	few parts present and clear	no parts present or clear
Primary Audience: Identified and accurate; cited if necessary	all parts present and clear	most parts present and clear	some parts present and clear	few parts present and clear	no parts present or clear
Thesis Statement: Answers both questions: main argument? rhetorical appeal(s)?	all parts present and clear	most parts present and clear	some parts present and clear	few parts present and clear	no parts present or clear
Assertions/Topic Sentences: Clearly expressed with necessary information?	all parts present and clear	most parts present and clear	some parts present and clear	few parts present and clear	no parts present or clear
Evidence: Uses enough examples, details, and quotes to support assertions	all parts present and clear	most parts present and clear	some parts present and clear	few parts present and clear	no parts present or clear
Rhetorical appeal: Relates to article and explained	present and clear	mostly present and clear	somewhat present and clear	unclear	absent
Evidence: Quotes selected, integrated, and commented upon clearly; cited using *MLA*, 8th ed.	all parts present and clear	most parts present and clear	some parts present and clear	few parts present and clear	no parts present or clear
Analysis: Explains how evidence supports Assertions; related to thesis	all parts present and clear	most parts present and clear	some parts present and clear	few parts present and clear	no parts present or clear
Conventions (25%)					
Format: 4/c style sheet; *TNR* font; title in your words; front of paper	all parts present and clear	most parts present and clear	some parts present and clear	few parts present and clear	no parts present or clear
Punctuated titles of newspaper/article correctly	Yes	Some	No		
Works Cited: cites article accurately; formatted correctly; proofread	Yes	Somewhat	No		
Diction: college-level/professional	All	Most	Some	Few	None

CHAPTER 4

Rubrics

> "Rubrics can act as wonderful translation devices. . . . Not only do they help . . . students understand what [instructors] are talking about, but they help [instructors] understand when and where our words are not being understood, or worse yet, are being completely misunderstood."—Dannelle D. Stevens and Antonia J. Levi, *Introduction to Rubrics*, 21

This chapter looks at the construction of rubrics as they relate to writing assignments and feedback. Many books about the construction of rubrics for a variety of purposes are on the market.

How Is "Rubric" Best Defined in Relation to Feedback?
　A rubric is a set of criteria with descriptions to show students' proficiency levels; they range from less to more detailed. They may be used as part of either formative or summative assessments, discussed in chapter 3. Rubrics act as "translation devices" to present different categories of comments; they also reveal patterns of positives and negatives in student performance, then inform instruction.

How Are Rubrics Categorized in Relation to Feedback?

1. Analytic: each criterion is assessed separately, and
2. Holistic: all criteria are assessed together.

Both promote inter-rater reliability (i.e., equity and fairness across students' performance).

What Are Common Rubrics?

Rubrics are performance scales, checklists, holistic, check minus/ check/check plus, and contracts.

What Are Common Experiences With Rubrics in High School and College Humanities Courses?

Instructors typically are familiar with rubrics because many schools, both high school and college, use standardized rubrics that the administration imposes to fit standards of learning. Some college humanities courses also have standardized rubrics. Instructors can benefit from becoming familiar with rubrics but still the need to customize them for each assignment according to instructors' purposes and feedback styles.

What Are Common Parts That Appear in the Grid (i.e., Rubrics)?

Scales are descriptive (e.g., "Excellent," "Above Average"), Yes/No checklists, grade letters, and numbers/percentages; *dimensions* are elements assessed (e.g., "Evidence"), *descriptions or criteria* are feedback (e.g., "limited analysis of quote"), and *weight of dimensions* (e.g., 40%, Evidence). The scales describe to what extent a student performed to expectations in dimensions as noted in instructors' descriptions.

How Are Descriptions in Rubrics Clarified in Relation to Feedback?

The goal is to coordinate instruction and assessment through consistent language of learning outcomes (objectives), rubrics, and comments. The more consistent the documents, the better students are able to understand and apply feedback in their writing. An example of a description is: "Reasoning is clear and supported with relevant details."

How Does Timing of Rubrics Relate to the Feedback Process?

Introduce them at the beginning of a writing assignment; again, "midstream," with the class and in peer reviews to remind students of the expectations and show gaps to fill in revisions; and, finally, toward the end of the process for students to do self-checks to ensure that they are striving to meet the learning objectives.

What Are Common Characteristics of Rubrics?

The common characteristics of rubrics include suitable, definable, observable, distinctive, and clear in terms of weight for sections and language. Many types of writing assignments in different humanities courses lend themselves to rubrics. Examples include research, analytical, rhetorical, response, and reflection papers. They can also extend to reports and summaries.

What Are the Pitfalls of Rubrics?
These include:

- mixing purpose,
- mismatched language of the classroom in lectures and discussions contradicting the vocabulary of rubric sections,
- focusing on elements not taught,
- side-stepping objectives, and
- conveying contradictory messages (e.g., students receive contradictory advice—conventions are 25%, yet 75% of comments relate to grammar/punctuation).

Rubrics should be consistent with commentary, matching weights of various criteria. Also, a rubric should not substitute for meaningful marginal and summation comments.

Are Rubrics Typically Used for Formative or Summative Assessment?
Often, summative assessment calls for checks for each criterion. However, rubrics used for formative assessment have value during peer reviews and discussion of expectations during the writing process. In summation, formative assessment is the descriptions, and summative assessment is the learning outcomes.

What Role Does Evaluation Play in Rubrics in Relation to Feedback?
Once descriptions are checked for each criterion, numerical scores and grades follow.

Which Elements of Writing Are Most Important and Relevant to Include in Rubrics for Nonfiction Writing?
These include the thesis (message), evidence, analysis, voice/style, conventions (including documentation of sources), audience awareness, and fulfillment of purpose.

44   CHAPTER 4

When Is It an Appropriate Time to Discuss Rubrics for Writing Assignments?

Discuss the rubric in class at the same time as introducing or posting (or both) the writing assignments. Ensure that students know that rubrics inform the writing process, and they can use them to set goals for their papers. Also, the foremost purpose of rubrics is to provide meaningful feedback, and, secondarily, to justify grades.

What Are Options for Performance Scales?

Table 4.1. Terms of Performance Scales

F	D	C	B	A
Poor	*Below Average*	*Average*	*Good*	*Excellent*
Unsatisfactory	Not Yet Competent	Partly Competent	Competent	Distinguished
Not Proficient	Not Yet Proficient or Novice	Nearing Proficiency	Proficient	Advanced
Unsatisfactory	Below Satisfactory	Satisfactory	Above Satisfactory	Well-Above Satisfactory
Below Standards	Novice	Intermediate	High Intermediate	Advanced
Below Standards	Beginning	Developing	Above Average	Accomplished
Below Benchmarks	Not Meeting Benchmarks	Benchmarks	Milestones	Capstones

What Are Features of Performance Indicators?

They fall between specific and general; consistent and clear. The following are some adjectives for descriptions:

- Strengths: analytical, aware, clear, comprehensive, consistent, convincing, creative, credible, developed, effective, engaging, focused, fulfilling, insightful, logical, reasoned, strategic
- Needs: basic, broad, confusing, illogical, impoverished, inaccurate, inappropriate incoherent, incomplete, insufficient, irrelevant, lacks, limited, repetitive, superficial, underdeveloped

What Do Rubrics Ultimately Convey?

They convey our values: writing as a process (content > style > editing), critical thinking, sharp reading comprehension, revision, audience awareness, and presentation. Rhetorically speaking, rubrics show what instructors emphasize in instruction and writing assignments (e.g., an in-depth analysis of evidence, which is conveyed in lessons).

SAMPLE RUBRICS

The following sample rubrics include Holistic for a Research Proposal and Performance Scales for Short Reflection Paper.

SAMPLE RUBRIC I. HOLISTIC FOR A RESEARCH PROPOSAL

Note: 25% Conventions ____; 25% Citations/Paraphrasing ____; 50% Content ____; Grade ___.

- A = Writer is in full command of topic; his/her voice is moderately audible in the commentary balanced well with facts/data; excellent evidence of critical thinking and advanced understanding of research; paper persuades selected audience of thesis; purpose achieved fully; thesis clearly outlines p, s, and b; thesis traced carefully through each area of proposal; problem is narrow in scope and includes topic/concluding sentences with strong explanation.
  In addition, solution is clear and feasible/benefits likewise; conclusion wraps up p, s, b with excellent reflection; incorporated and introduced quotes/paraphrases; drew mainly from primary sources; balanced sources among different authors and sites; excellent paraphrasing; advanced vocabulary; correct format and minimal to no grammatical/spelling errors; paper exceeds expectations.
- B = Writer is in full command of topic; his/her voice is moderately audible in the commentary balanced well with facts/data; very good evidence of good critical thinking and solid research; paper persuades selected audience of thesis; purpose achieved; thesis clearly outlines p, b, and s, though one area could be greater emphasized; thesis traced carefully through each area of proposal; problem is narrow in scope and includes topic/

concluding sentences with strong depth of explanation, but they could extend; solution is clear and feasible/benefits likewise.

In addition, conclusion wraps up p, s, b with good reflection; incorporated and introduced quotes/paraphrases, though 1–2 need more attn.; drew mainly from primary sources; balanced sources among different authors and sites; above-average paraphrasing and quoting; advanced vocabulary; correct format and minimal grammar/spelling errors; paper meets expectations; one more draft.

C = Writer is in mixed command of topic; his/her mixed voice is barely and moderately audible in the commentary balanced with some facts/data; average evidence of critical thinking and solid research; paper somewhat persuades selected audience of thesis; purpose achieved somewhat; thesis outlines p, b, and/or s—more clarity; p, b, s not aligned as well as expected; problem/solution are too narrow and/or broad, and consistent topic/concluding sentences needed; conclusion wraps up p, s, b with average reflection.

In addition, student incorporated and introduced some quotes/paraphrases; drew mainly from secondary sources; somewhat balanced sources among different authors and sites; some concerning paraphrasing and quoting, but not plagiarized; shows some understanding of research; need more advanced vocabulary; correct format, but a pattern of grammatical/spelling errors; paper falls somewhat below expectations; two more drafts.

D = Writer is not in full command of topic; his/her voice is barely audible in the commentary imbalanced with facts/data; low evidence of critical thinking and solid research; paper doesn't truly persuade selected audience of thesis; purpose achieved unevenly; thesis needs to outline p, b, and s clearly; p, b, and s not aligned; thesis not traced carefully through each area of proposal; problem is too broad or narrow in scope and doesn't include all topic/concluding sentences and evidence with strong depth of explanation.

In addition, solution is not clear and feasible; benefits likewise; conclusion wraps up p, s, b with little reflection; need to better incorporate and introduce quotes/paraphrases; drew mainly from secondary sources; imbalance of sources among different authors and sites; poor understanding of paraphrasing; vocabulary below; incorrect format and too many grammatical and/or spelling errors; paper falls below expectations; three more drafts.

Areas to Improve:

Content:

_____Problem needs more depth/focus

_____Solution needs more depth/focus

_____Benefits need more depth/focus

Paraphrasing/Quoting:

_____ Paraphrases are too close to original source

_____ Paraphrases need more length

_____ Too many secondary sources

_____ Leaning too heavily on 1–2 sources rather than balancing all 5

_____ Quote numbers/stats

Conventions:

_____ Series of comma errors

_____ Word count

_____ MLA style needs attention to detail

SAMPLE RUBRIC II. PERFORMANCE SCALE FOR SHORT REFLECTION PAPER

Note: Assignment in chapter 2.

Table 4.2. Rubric for Short Reflection Paper

	Unsatisfactory	Below Satisfactory	Satisfactory	Above Satisfactory	Well-Above Satisfactory
Thesis					
Major Supporting Points					
Minor Supporting Points					
Quotes: Selection and Integration					
Terms from Class					
Academic Diction					
Conclusion					

	Unsatisfactory	Below Satisfactory	Satisfactory	Above Satisfactory	Well-Above Satisfactory
Format of Paper					
MLA Style for Quotes					
Quotes Introduced					
Transitions					
Grammar/Punctuation					
Other					

Content (75%)

Conventions (25%)

What did you do effectively?

Which areas do you need to improve upon in future papers?

Grade: _____

CHAPTER 5

Commenting Vocabulary

"Instructors are challenged by the contradiction of being an ally as they teach and an adversary as they grade."—Peter Elbow, "Embracing Contraries in the Teaching Process," 333

By serving as students' ally, instructors take on the role of "coaches" who hold a steady belief that students can grow as writers—with their constructive, steady guidance.

Now that we have covered the feedback process, writing assignments, assessment, and rubrics, and we have now reached the "heart" of this text, the content turns to a key component of actual comments. This chapter provides a list of potential comments as a reference for instructors who may need fresh ways to comment on students' papers.

MAIN TENETS FOR COMMENTING ON STUDENTS' PAPERS

What Is the Main Tenet for Providing Feedback?
Don't replace the student's intentions (or purpose) as a writer with intentions as instructors as responders.

What Is a Framework for the Feedback Process?

- First, focus on content and organization.
- Second, focus on style.
- Third, focus on editing at sentence level.

What Is at Issue With Commenting on Students' Papers?

Paradoxically, we write seemingly infinite comments, yet our students read only a finite number of them. If our commenting becomes excessive (i.e., marking and cataloging every error) we become our students' copy editors, which results in minimal impact on their writing development. Further, ownership of the paper shifts from students to instructors. Different stages of the drafting process require various levels and types of instructor guidance: the extent to which instructors assess papers and offer directive comments for revisions; the way in which they present; the way in which they act as an audience; how much to say; and when to be directive.

What Is the Main Issue With Correcting Errors at the Sentence and Word Levels?

Repeatedly correcting these errors is akin to pushing the elevator button multiple times—they are futile attempts to show students their mistakes without any impact.

What Is the Main Objective of Using Commenting Vocabulary?

It is engaging students in the feedback process, specifically their actions to address global or larger issues for revisions; also to examine the content (what?) and tone (how?) of comments. The form of the comments strongly influences the function and meaning of the comments: Form → Content → Voice → Diction and Tone.

What Role Do Instructors' Good Intentions Play in the Feedback Process?

The feedback road is usually paved with good intentions—both from instructors and students. Yet, the road is rocky sometimes with mismatched intentions and perceptions. Because time is *always* of the essence in any writing-based classroom, the feedback process can become less burdensome, and communication can improve so that intentions do not overshadow actions but instead, match them.

Instructors indicate what is working and what needs improvement in writing; they show how students' arguments are or are not addressing their primary audiences. So, what does improving learning through assessment depend on? It depends on commentary that educates and motivates students to develop as writers.

What Are the Main Roles of Instructors Providing Commentary?

They serve as a "primary audience of one" who represents the wider primary audiences to whom students are directing their arguments. They engage students in a dialogue—rather than a monologue—to affirm their work and help them understand how they can improve clarity, organization, development, and more in their papers.

Their main role is that of audience of one who asks questions, expresses confusion or uncertainty, recommends edits, and praises strengths. Overall, they respond to the student writer's meaning—coaxing out implicit meaning and affirming explicit meaning are most effective.

Students may begin to see themselves as hunters searching only for what we want them to do rather than emerging academic writers who need to develop their own voices. After scanning comments, students are sometimes left confused about their priority and exactly how to address them in revisions.

On final drafts (without revision opportunities), students may see comments as neither urgent nor relevant, but rather *only* justification of grades (rather than meaningful comments to help them grow as writers); therefore, they may not take comments as seriously or transfer them to subsequent writing assignments.

Sometimes, comments are used for summative purposes *and* to justify grades. It is best if students understand the purpose of the comments and *how* they may use comments meaningfully in either revision or subsequent drafts.

Students want us to read their papers for meaning, rather than as a chain of many errors that convey the message that the only road to higher grades is to correct all errors. That may lead to unmet expectations. By providing meaningful, useful comments about major issues such as a brief thesis or inadequate evidence, students may see that we are reading their arguments meaningfully rather than superficially. This is not to say that sentence-level issues are not important but, rather, best addressed toward the end of the writing process.

Why Don't Students Use Instructors' Feedback on Subsequent Papers?
Students . . .

- are caught in a sizable gap between instructors' intentions and students' perceptions
- are engulfed with many comments and are unable to discern priorities (all comments look like priorities); they read partial information and ignore the remainder
- are loyal to past English teacher's comments because addressing them led to above-average grades
- are not equipped to make meaning out of the comments, especially complex ones with mixed purposes
- are not yet capable of assimilating feedback
- are self-immunized against negative feedback
- do not read comments (or cannot read them due to illegible handwriting) and focus only on grades
- have an emotional response (e.g., anger and frustration) that blocks understanding and application
- have had many summative, rather than formative, assessments (on rough drafts), so they are conditioned to focus on grades
- have reading comprehension challenges and simply do not understand the comments
- see comments as distant or unrelated to classroom discussions and assignments

Why, Specifically, Don't Students Address (or Minimally Address) Sentence-Level Issues?
Students . . .

- do not see value in them
- do not focus on them; instead, they focus on bigger content issues
- have low audience awareness skills
- do not understand (or forgot) fundamental grammar, usage, and punctuation rules and how to apply them

How Do We Know if Instructors' Commentary Is Effective?

Students understand and use feedback in revision of papers. Their writing becomes increasingly responsive to their primary audiences. Yet, teaching the rhetorical situation remains an elusive process, which does raise the question that looms over the English classroom: Is there a quantifiable way to measure the efficacy of a feedback process? Many instructors are being asked to document their methods via quantifiable assessments, which may result in either a useful reflection or resentment of having to "check a box."

However, taking the opportunity to track one's comments across a sampling of papers does, in fact, reveal emphasis and values conveyed in areas that instructors believe are important for students to address (e.g., extend and clarify argument in thesis statements). It is eye-opening to take a closer look at the frequency and type of comments so that instructors can make adjustments as needed for more impactful commentary.

Which Type of Balance Is Necessary to Strike in Approaching Commentary?

Balance authoritative with interactive; conversational with formal; and facilitative with directive. In summation, offer well-developed specific responses in a conversational style so that students practice their own decisions as writers with their instructors' guidance.

Many types of comments are common in feedback practices such as evaluations, open-ended/close-ended questions, positive comments, clarifications, understandings, misunderstandings, reflections, responses, advice, praise, critique, and explanations. Of all the different types of comments, reader-based interpretations are quite effective at helping students keep ownership of their words and self-assess their progress.

What Are Various Types of Comments?

The many types of comments include advice, checks, clarifications, close-ended questions, directives, explanations, facilitative, open-ended questions, praise, reflections, and understandings. See figure 5.1 for which type of comment is recommended more than others.

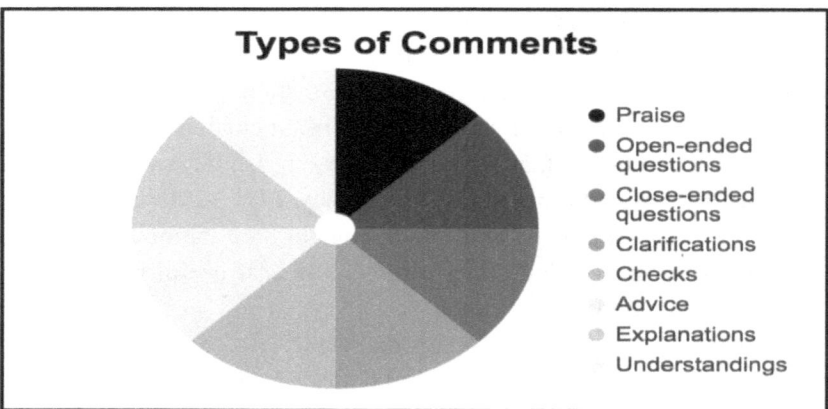

Figure 5.1. Types of Comments. *Author created*

For a balanced approach to feedback, see figure 5.2.

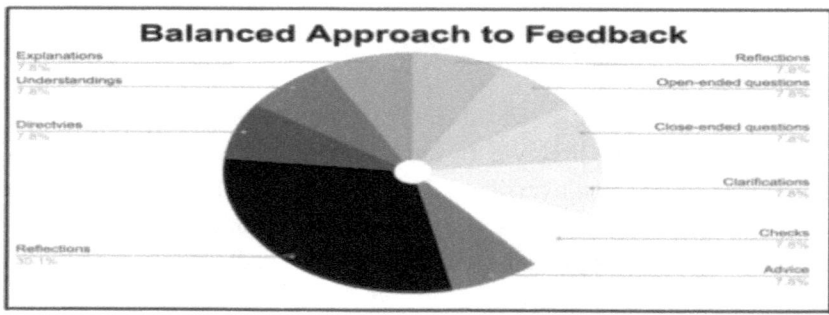

Figure 5.2. A Balanced Approach to Feedback. *Author created*

What Is a Useful Approach to Commentary?

Use the acronym DID, which translates to **D**raw attention to the issue/diagnose; **I**dentify strengths and/or needs; **D**escribe next steps. In other words, what is the problematic area? Why is the area strong or deficient? Which steps are necessary to take in revisions?

A good question for instructors to ask themselves is how they can transform commentary so that fewer mismatches between their intentions and students' perceptions result. Taking a closer look at a random sample of instructors' commentary using the columns below and tracing several comments from "General" to "Better" to "Even Better" can promote reflection on ways to communicate more clearly. Instructors could show students this table and ask them if they perceive the most useful comments for revision.

General:	Better:	Even Better:
Be more specific	Unclear point	Unclear point about ____.
Too brief	Be more specific about ____.	Add more details about ____ to fully explore why ____ is ____.
Revise	Add more details about ____.	Revise this paragraph by adding details about ____, then analyze why these details are relevant to ____. ____ makes more sense.

VAGUE VERSUS SPECIFIC COMMENTS

The difference between vague or specific comments is that vague comments are a waste of precious time whereas specific comments are productive and may lead to more precise revisions. The following are examples of both:

1a. Sentence: The tennis player returned to the hospital where she had undergone emergency surgery on her Achilles tendon last year.

   Vague comment: Huh? When?

1b. [Last year], the tennis player returned to the hospital where she had undergone emergency surgery on her Achilles tendon.

   Specific comment: Relocating a misplaced adverb phrase shows clear answer to question: When?

2a. Sentence: Tan's essay, "Mother Tongue," is best summarizes as a humble experience about the English language; it's not "broken," but different and worthy of respect.

   Vague comment: Wrong words

   s-v: summarized

2b. Tan's essay, "Mother Tongue," is best <u>summarized</u> as a humble experience about the
                      spell out: it is

    English language; <u>it's</u> not "broken," but different and worthy of respect.

    Specific comment: identify errors show correct word/phrasing near faulty words/phrases.

3a. Sentence: Even today, we still found ourselves in a challenging time with the virus and a need to stay home, away from others, and to social distance, with masks.

    Vague comment: Awkward and wordy

3b. Even today, we still found ourselves living in a challenging time due to the virus, ~~with the virus~~ needing to stay home, ~~away~~ social distancing from others, ~~with~~ and wearing masks. [Instructor would use the strikethrough to show excessive, unnecessary words and adding parallelism]

    Specific comment: Eliminate unnecessary words; focus on nouns and verbs

What Are Specific Verbs Helpful in Commenting on Students' Papers?

- acknowledge
- address
- analyze
- argue
- assert
- claim
- clarify
- contend
- demonstrate
- develop
- emphasize
- employ
- exemplifies
- illustrate
- indicate
- observe
- prove
- recommend
- report
- reveal
- suggest
- support

COMMENTING VOCABULARY

What Is a "Commenting Vocabulary"?

Commenting vocabulary consists of comments that instructors have tailored to each student's writing. However, it can be helpful to have templates and sample phrases to draw upon. Even veteran instructors who have ritual feedback practices can benefit from shaking up their comments. Below is a list of commenting vocabulary that balances facilitative and directive feedback divided into these categories: Praise, Questions, and Constructive Feedback.

Praise

Overall Argument

- Good work overall with _____ and _____.
- Great hook. I want to keep reading.
- I notice your effort, which has led to success with _____.
- You have aspired to (and met) objectives of assignment.
- You have demonstrated that you know how to learn, form an argument, or _____.
- You showed grit and resilience when faced with this challenging writing assignment.
- You have stepped up since our conference, and the result is _____.
- You've experimented with a new style, and it has paid dividends for understanding and interest.

Primary Audience Awareness

- Formality of tone and style are appropriate for primary audience.
- Good sensory description about _____, which will appeal to your primary audience.
- The chief strength of your argument is _____, which will appeal to your primary audience.
- You showed respect for your primary audience by _____.
- Your grammar/punctuation/usage are well-edited for your primary audience.
- Your primary audience will respond particularly to _____.

Message or Thesis

- You've revealed important truth(s) about _____, which contributes to a sounder argument.
- Your thesis helps your primary audience to understand your position on topic.
- Your thesis is defensible and relevant.
- Your thesis is persuasive about _____ for your primary audience.

Evidence and Analysis

Evidence

- Evidence is unified about one subtopic.
- Evidence supports the topic sentence/thesis.
- Fine interpretation of evidence here.
- Good detail to show _____.
- The image of _____ works well here.
- This evidence is effective because _____.
- You have a solid bank of examples to support your topic sentences.

Analysis

- Analysis is well-balanced with evidence.
- Analysis ties back to the thesis clearly.
- Insightful observations.
- Well-observed details.
- What can you do to increase depth in your paper?

Questions

Overall

- Are you implying _____?
- How can you add value to _____?
- How challenging was this argument for you to accomplish?
- What can I do to support you?
- What exactly are you trying to achieve in this paper?

Primary Audience Awareness

- How can data about your primary audience (e.g., race, gender, education) drive your argument?
- How can you be certain your primary audience knows all this information about _____ without explanation?
- How can you use more _____ to fully engage your primary audience?
- How do you think you come across to your primary audience in this sentence/paragraph/essay?
- Whom do you envision as the primary audience of your argument?

Message or Thesis

- Can you explain to me the logic of your argument?
- Have you considered the opposite point of view? How would you respond to a counterargument? Do you have evidence to support the counterargument? What is the counterargument to explain in evidence?
- How can you expand your thesis to also answer How? or Why?
- How can you narrow your thesis from multiple topics to one major arguable one?
- How does _____ enhance or impede your argument?
- Is the argument about _____ really an either/or argument? How can you introduce more flexible thinking, given your primary audience?
- What else can you say about your position on _____?
- What exactly are you trying to say about _____?

Evidence and Analysis

Evidence

- Can you find a better way to get at this contrast/comparison?
- Can you provide a definition?
- How can you develop this/these points further to support your thesis?

- How can you use evidence more systematically to link to your thesis?
- How can you use more credible data to support your topic sentences (or claims or assertions)?
- Illustrating more specific examples about _____ would add clarity/interest/understanding.
- In which way do these sentences/paragraphs/sections support or not support your thesis?
- Several of the explanations about _____ could have been rendered more vividly.

Analysis

- How can you extend your thinking to answer How? or Why? evidence is relevant and supportive of your thesis?
- Why have you discussed _____ here, rather than _____ where it is more persuasive (or logical)?
- Why is the point about _____ significant/relevant?
- You have given primarily a summary. Why? You can assert your point of view with evidence to support it.

Constructive Feedback

Overall

- _____ doesn't fit the requirement for _____.
- _____ only led to marginal improvements in _____.
- _____ would make more of an impact for _____.
- _____ needs retooling for greater impact.
- Be open to cultivate learning more about _____.
- Be sure you have a solid understanding about _____ before you revise your draft.
- Before starting a second (or third) draft, I recommend a reverse outline to increase logical progression throughout the argument.
- By concentrating on the secondary topic about _____, you are abandoning your primary topic. Recenter your argument back on your primary topic.

- Despite several strengths, your argument needs _____.
- Despite these strengths, your argument does not hold weight about _____.
- Give more thought to how you want to shape your argument about _____.
- I don't understand whether you understood _____.
- I don't understand what you meant by _____.
- I have these concerns: _____, and I'm optimistic that you can overcome them.
- I know you're a more capable writer than you're showing here.
- Start again.
- Step back from your experiences/explanation and decide on a different direction or specifics to tie back to your thesis.
- The assignment calls for _____ rather than _____.
- This essay reads as a first draft (or rush job). Revise it while addressing my comments.
- This is not of passing quality. I expect more at this stage of the writing process.

Primary Audience Awareness

- _____ shows a pattern of errors about _____ that inhibit easy reading.
- A series of _____ (grammar/punctuation/usage) errors distract from your argument, and your primary audience may stop reading.
- Avoiding casual/colloquial/slang language inappropriate to your primary audience.
- Choose words that are more likely to persuade your audience of your position.
- Clue your primary audience in on _____.
- Define unfamiliar terms for your primary audience.
- Despite assignment to write for an opposing audience, you have written for a supportive one and imposed your own views in a slanted way. Writing for an opposing audience is more challenging and beneficial because you have to think through your own argument/position carefully.

- Does _____ help your primary audience's understanding of _____?
- Errors of _____ are impeding your primary audience's understanding of _____.
- I suspect your audience will understand your point of view because _____.
- Improve transitions to assist your primary audience's connections/understandings within the paragraph or between paragraphs.
- Introduce _____ more engagingly for your audience.
- Make the meaning of these sentences clearer for your primary audience.
- You need to return to the assignment—you're straying too far from guidelines.

Message or Thesis

- A clearer way to state your argument involves _____.
- Your argument doesn't have a direction. Clarify _____.
- Carefully managing the vocabulary in your thesis allows for greater persuasive power.
- Extend your thesis to answer "How?" or "Why?" for greater complexity and clarity.
- Help me to understand _____.
- I am confused by your word choice of _____.
- Improve _____ first, then look at _____.
- Relocate the last sentence(s) to _____ for greater effectiveness.
- Resist the urge to focus on more than one topic (or too broad/narrow a topic).
- Although _____ is true, _____ is more relevant because _____.
- You have 2–3 theses in one. Focus on one major arguable topic.
- You have two arguments: one is sound; the other is shaky.
- You haven't mentioned the main issue in this controversy.
- You're using very general language, so it is hard to know your true meaning.

Evidence and Analysis

Evidence

- Add more explanation about _____ to fully develop your point.
- Avoid _____ without specific examples.
- Comment further on the advantages/disadvantages of _____.
- Consider omitting _____ altogether.
- The evidence is too lengthy; making _____ more concise would add value.
- The main issue is not supporting your assertions with evidence.
- This evidence is not enough to guarantee an effective argument.
- You're expecting your evidence to be self-evident.
- Your evidence assumes understanding of _____.
- Your evidence is subordinated to the minor, rather than major, part of your thesis.
- Your evidence is underdeveloped and lacking in specifics.
- Your facts do not support your thesis.

Analysis

- I'm not clear on your analysis point about _____.
- I'm unclear what _____ refers to analytically.
- Quote/paraphrase from credible sources.
- Rephrase _____ for clarity. Your primary audience would not understand _____ otherwise.
- Analyze subpoints more in-depth.
- Take more time to read/interpret _____.
- The argument against _____ is significant because _____; clarify this relationship.
- This sentence(s) doesn't belong in this paragraph _____.
- Too much summary; not enough analysis.
- Try rearranging _____ for greater effect/clarity.
- You fell short here: _____.
- You have not argued convincingly and analytically about _____.
- You lost me there—I cannot follow your analysis.

- Identify the opposing argument; explain why your argument is more persuasive.
- Analyze why the opposing argument is inaccurate, filled with logical fallacies, false, or otherwise faulty.

COMMENTING ON CONVENTIONS: GRAMMAR, PUNCTUATION, AND USAGE

What can instructors do about correcting errors at the sentence and word levels? How do they move away from the role of "censor in chief"? Correcting every error (or the majority of them) seems to have little positive impact on students' sentence-level issues (as shown by student papers in this text). This experience leaves us fatigued if we routinely adopt editorial roles, and it sends this message: we are our students' copy editors, shifting the ownership from students to their instructors. If this is the reality, instructors are thwarting students' self-discovery as writers.

Instead, we want them to become self-editors (which is a process), not rely heavily on online programs that correct grammatical and punctuation errors for them. This "stem-the-tide" approach guides students—repetitively and consistently—to pay attention to their errors and take the opportunity to correct them. The soundest advice is to focus mainly on students' errors that impede the primary audience's understanding.

Conventions for Any Section

Note: See the next few pages for further approaches to conventions.

- Edit the next draft with a particular eye on punctuation.
- I noted 4–6 areas of faulty punctuation/grammar; examine carefully and rewrite correctly on the next draft(s). All may lead to one more sentence-level problem.
- Remember the value of proofreading and editing.
- Rephrase this sentence/phrase to clarify _____.
- See if you understand how the semicolon or comma is used here, and why.
- Try combining sentences for less wordiness.

- Use transition words from paragraph to paragraph, or within paragraphs.
- Your purpose and effect on the primary audience are distorted with too many errors.

What Alternatives Teach Students to Become Efficient Self-Editors?
Guide students to . . .

- use resources: peers, handbooks, tutors at writing centers, online writing sites, and more
- keep an editing Word file in which they would . . .
  - copy faulty sentences from subsequent papers
  - correct faulty sentences and accompany them with rules (from website or handbook)
  - reference when writing future papers
  - reflect on patterns and set goals to avoid errors in future papers
  - report on patterns/errors they have endeavored to avoid in submitted papers (include on separate pages submitted with final drafts)

What Are More Reasonable Approaches to Marking and Correcting Errors—With More Impact?

FOCUS ON PATTERNS AND THREE-STEP APPROACH

1. Focus on patterns, rather than each individual error; bring students' attention to these patterns as they may not be aware of them.
2. Create a list of abbreviations that identify errors; ask students to refer to the list when reading your corrections. Encourage language of commentary in class discussions.
3. Use a multi-step approach that draws attention to errors:
   - 1st time: Identify and correct error.
   - 2nd time: Identify error with abbreviation.
   - 3rd time: Identify error with only a circle.
   - 4+ time(s): Not identifying or correcting error; students should seek help from resources or self-editing practice.

Example:

- 1st time: Identify and correct errors
    - Students bought clothing, and they collected money for the homeless at Thanksgiving.
- 2nd time: Identify error with abbreviation; if the error occurs on the same page, circle and draw lines between them to show the pattern
    - Students raised $400 from a car wash and they donated the money to a local homeless shelter.
- 3rd time: Identify error with only a circle (circle placed above homeless)
    - Students learned about the plight of the homeless in their hometown and they decided to start a fundraiser to support them.
- 4+ time(s): Neither identify nor correct error; student corrects subsequent errors

LIST OF COMMON ERRORS

Avoid identifying and correcting errors in students' rough drafts; instead, generate either a list of common errors or faulty sentences with errors (one from each student's paper for the sake of equity) and correct them together in class. An alternative is for peer groups to each correct three faulty sentences and share the results with the class in a slide or on a flipchart paper. Next, give students opportunities to correct specified errors in their rough drafts. Hold them accountable for only these errors, listing them in an editing file, then set individual (or class) goals to conquer only these errors.

PEER DIVISION OF LABOR FOR EDITING DIFFERENT PARTS OF DRAFTS

Ask students to bring in 3–4 copies of rough drafts. Distribute to one peer group (not to include the writers) who divide up the writers' introduction, evidence, and other sections. After they have corrected the errors, discuss them as a group, noting common errors/patterns. Repeat the process with another round of drafts until every student in class has received a thorough review of his or her errors.

Writers ultimately are responsible for correcting errors in each section and applying "lessons learned" in their final papers. This activity fits into the middle of the writing process with a focus only on one section of students' papers that they can comprehend and apply to other sections of their final drafts.

RETURN PAPERS WITHOUT GRADES TO FOCUS ON COMMENTARY

If students have not applied the lessons of this editing process and taken their instructors' convention comments seriously, consider returning those papers with either no grade or a low grade and require them to edit their paper for resubmission (and potentially, a higher grade).

EDITING LOGS

Guide students to keep an editing log of their common errors and the sentences in which they appear—for subsequent papers. They can refer to the log prior to writing final drafts to ensure that they have addressed these common errors.

SENTENCE-LEVEL EXERCISE AFTER RETURNING FINAL DRAFTS

Since students tend to pay attention to content-driven feedback, they do not tend to focus on convention comments. This exercise places the spotlight on conventions, especially at the sentence level, that show up in research papers (sample in text) or other writing assignments. The main purpose of this exercise is to raise awareness so students do not keep repeating the same errors, and to manage edits more effectively in revisions or future papers.

Directions: Select 8–10 conventions (sentence-level, citation, and formatting errors to cut and paste below, then correct them).
Example: Period outside quotes when no citation follows:

> Original: . . . there are numerous variations of the language distinct from what some would consider standard "American English".
> Corrected: . . . there are numerous variations of the language distinct from what some would consider standard "American English."

1.
2.
3.
4.
5.
6.
7.
8.
9.
10.

"THE TWENTY MOST COMMON STUDENT ERRORS" APPROACH

In 1993, rhetoric and composition researchers Connors and Lunsford examined twenty-one thousand student papers and generated a list of the 20 most common errors (Connors and Lunsford 1988, 400). They include *sentence-level errors* (e.g., fragments and missing commas) and *word-level errors* (e.g., spelling and wrong word).

Below is a list of acronyms to accompany the "Common Errors." Share them with students, using the acronyms for marking errors in their writing, and ask peer reviewers to do the same.

1. Missing comma after an introductory element: phrase or other group of words (MCIE)

   Incorrect: In the dining hall we ate diverse foods to satisfy our hunger pains.
   Correct: In the dining hall, we ate diverse foods to satisfy our hunger pains.

2. Vague personal pronoun reference (P Ref)

   Incorrect: *Juan and Diego* presented their research findings. *He* provided useful information about sustainable energy places.
   Correct: *Juan and Diego* presented their research findings. *They* provided their useful findings about sustainable energy places.

3. Missing comma in a compound sentence (C in CS)

   Incorrect: Abigail and I stopped at the coffee shoppe and we enjoyed hot cocoa on a cold day.
   Correct: Abigail and I stopped at the coffee shoppe, and we enjoyed hot cocoa on a cold day.

4. Wrong word (WW)

   Incorrect: Deciding *weather* or not to request course validation, Paula consulted her college adviser.
   Correct: Deciding *whether* or not to request course validation, Paula consulted her college adviser.

5. Missing comma(s) after a nonrestrictive element (CNRE)

   Incorrect: The garden filled with various vegetables, including peppers and cucumbers paid dividends during the middle of our summer-school session.
   Correct: The garden filled with various vegetables, including peppers and cucumbers, paid dividends during the middle of our summer-school session.

6. Wrong or missing verb ending (VE)

   Incorrect: Last spring, Donovan *wins* the fashion-design award for his spectacular work.
   Correct: Last spring, Donovan *won* the fashion-design award for his spectacular work.

7. Wrong or missing preposition (Prep)

   Incorrect: *To* the front of the room, Julie took her seat on the environmental ethics panel.
   Correct: *In* the front of the room, Julie took her seat on the environmental ethics panel.

8. Comma splice (CS)

   Incorrect: Jamal skied the Black Diamond mountains he showed his expert skills to manage the danger factor.
   Correct: Jamal skied the Back Diamond mountains; he showed his expert skills to manage the danger factor.

9. Missing or misplaced possessive apostrophe (MA)

   Incorrect: We registered for the *Womens'* Studies courses in advance because many students wanted to learn about *womens* rights (or lack thereof) in the eighteenth and nineteenth centuries.
   Correct: We registered for the *Women's* Studies courses in advance because many students wanted to learn about *women's* rights (or lack thereof) in the eighteenth and nineteenth centuries.

10. Unnecessary shift in tense (Tense)

    Incorrect: When *faced* with minimal time to finish taxes, Francina and Bettina had *planned* to help each other to complete them.
    Correct: When *faced* with minimal time to finish taxes, Francina and Bettina *would* help each other complete them.

11. Unnecessary shift in pronoun (Prn)

    Incorrect: *Students* scheduled the march for higher work-study salaries, and *you* need to meet by the student union by 8:00 a.m., or *we* will have to leave without *you*.
    Correct: *Students* scheduled the march for higher work-study salaries, and *they* need to meet by the student union by 8:00 a.m., or *we* will have to leave without *them*.

12. Sentence fragment (Frag)

    Incorrect: Which is why they waited in the wings until their names were called.
    Correct: They waited in the wings until their names were called.

13. Wrong tense or verb form (VF)

    Incorrect: During our holiday break, we *were volunteering* at a soup kitchen in Boston.
    Correct: During our holiday break, we *volunteered* at a soup kitchen in Boston.

14. Lack of agreement between subject and verb (S-V Ag)

    Incorrect: Neither the *professor* nor *her teaching assistant are* available on Thursday.
    Correct: Neither the *professor* nor *her teaching assistant is* available on Thursday.

15. Missing comma in a series (C in S). (For these sentences, employ the Oxford comma.)

    Incorrect: During the last few weeks of the semester, we took exams, wrote papers and delivered speeches.
    Correct: During the last few weeks of the semester, we took exams, wrote papers, and delivered speeches.

16. Lack of agreement between pronoun and antecedent (Prn. An)

    Incorrect: After lacrosse practice, *each player* took *their* equipment and drove home.
    Correct: After lacrosse practice, *each player* took *her* equipment and drove home.

Or

> After lacrosse practice, the players took their equipment and drove home.

17. Unnecessary comma(s) with a restrictive element (UCRE)

    Incorrect: The film, *Once Upon a Time in Hollywood*, was shown in McAllister Hall last week.
    Correct: The film *Once Upon a Time in Hollywood* was shown in McAllister Hall last week.

18. Fused sentence (FS)

    Incorrect: Some students remembered to bring their vaccination records others forgot to bring them.
    Correct: Some students remembered to bring their vaccination records; others forgot to bring them.

19. Dangling or misplaced modifier (DM or MM)

    Incorrect: Walking down the street, the bank is on the corner.
    Correct: The bank, which I noticed as I was driving by, is on the corner of Main and Smith streets.

20. Its/it's confusion (It's, Its)

    Incorrect: The tiger stalked *it's* prey, and *it's* a startling scene to watch from afar.
    Correct: The tiger stalked *its* prey, and *it is* a startling scene to watch from afar.

Following the discussion about purpose of comments, the next chapter addresses the need for careful design of writing assignments.

CHAPTER 6

Written Commentary

"Teachers' written feedback plays an essential role in a student's writing process. It helps students identify their own strengths and weaknesses, which, in case of the latter, will make students know how to go about improving themselves and become effective writers."—Penaflorida, "The Role of Teacher in Written Feedback—UK Essays," 364

The Goals of Commentary—Audio and Written—Include the Following:

1. students' accurate understanding and perceptions of their instructors' intentions behind comments
2. their increased ability to address comments in revisions usefully
3. further writing assignments to become more effective writers for their primary audiences.

COMPONENTS OF WRITTEN COMMENTARY

What Is a Useful Approach to Responding With Written Comments?
Less is more. Focus on 3-4 areas to comment on and save the focus on smaller errors for later in the writing process. Handwritten comments on papers versus typed comments online differ in their purposes in three ways: legibility, length, and load. For the purposes of this text, the advice is relevant to both handwritten comments on hard copies and typed comments (comment function, track changes, and posts) for papers posted online.

In terms of alignment, the more consistent use of language in the classroom, writing assignment, rubric, and commentary, the more positive the impact on student writing development as well as increased chances of students feeling less defeated and more engaged in the feedback process.

What Is Problematic With Written Comments?

Misunderstandings occur because of mismatches between instructors' intentions and students' perceptions. Further, rarely are there opportunities to negotiate these misunderstandings, which can appear again in the next writing assignment and feedback process. Sometimes, instructors' intentions are only to evaluate what is "wrong" in papers; as a result, students' perceptions are that "my instructor doesn't like my writing," "I guess I didn't do much right in this paper," or "I'm not good at writing." This sets back writing progress and creates a river of resentment in the classroom.

Alternative words for revision include reworking, changing, improving, developing, correcting, adjusting, altering, expanding, elaborating, amending, and transforming drafts.

Which Approach Holds Students Accountable for Reading and Understanding Instructors' Written Comments?

Instructors can walk around while students read their instructors' comments. Students check the comments they understand and plan to address in revisions. If they do not understand comments, students write a check minus, then discuss them with instructors at a different time. In a virtual classroom, students can work in breakout groups while the instructor visits each group, completing the same exercise as in the classroom.

STRENGTHS AND NEEDS LIST FROM RHETORICAL ANALYSIS WRITING ASSIGNMENT

Note: Approximately 80% of students demonstrated these strengths and needs.

Strengths

Note: Alphabetized; not in ranking order.

- explained rhetorical appeals with examples
- introductions
- invention worksheets
- quote sandwiches
- thesis statements
- titles
- understanding articles

Needs

Note: Alphabetized; not in ranking order.

- analyzing rhetorically (audiences and purposes)
- college-level vocabulary (mixing with casual words/slang)
- complex topic sentences
- conclusion (too brief; afterthought)
- format of citation format and works cited
- punctuating titles of literature
- punctuation
- transitions

COMMON COMMENTS: PATTERNS IN FEEDBACK

What did you do well on synthesis paper?

- most titles—creative and related to thesis
- opening sentences—capture audience's attention

- most thesis statements (full and answered prompt; followed, too)
- most topic sentences (included topic and answer to How? or Why?)
- details from story
- some analysis paragraphs
- some synthesis paragraphs
- most quote sandwiches (if partial, bottom slices left off)
- selection of quotes
- concluding paragraphs

What was a mixed performance on paper #2?

- some analysis paragraphs (too short or contained too many points)
- some synthesis paragraphs (contrasted one point/repetitive)
- works cited (missing information, no caps)

What did you need to improve upon in paper #2?

- introductory paragraphs (too short/too few lines about story to refresh audience)
- capitalization of proper/specific nouns (e.g., Communism)
- commas (not enough)
- diction (it, thing, ended up, talks about, and being)
- citation of quotes (Ojito 217). or Ojito explained, ". . . (217).
- other: analysis and synthesis

For the taxonomies shown in this chapter, which principles apply for greater effectiveness?

- Instructors' comments tend to be implicit or explicit—but not both.
- Instructors' written comments are broken down into singular points.
- Intentions are typically singular in expression.
- Students' perceptions tend to be reactionary (written without deep reflection), expressing one or several points.

TAXONOMIES

Students can complete taxonomies after reading and reflecting on instructors' written and audio feedback. They may set up a taxonomy that includes these areas. See chapter 7, tables 7.1 and 7.2, for a sample.

Students	Instructors' Written Comments	Students' Perceptions	Students' Plans to Address (or Not/Explain) in Revision	Instructor's Assessment

Note: These taxonomies are from the author's doctoral dissertation of a case study about negotiating meaning between instructors' intentions and students' perceptions.

Assignment #1: Write a research paper on a debatable topic in which you take a position and argue with credible evidence to persuade your primary audience to support your stance.

Table 6.1. Taxonomy of Instructor's Intentions and Students' Perceptions of Written Commentary for Assignment #1

Students	Instructor's Written Comments	Students' Perceptions	Students' Plans to Address (or Not/Explain) in Revision	Instructor's Assessment
Juanita	Add more analysis points to this section; explain how your facts about BLM are important and relate to the second part of your thesis that necessary change in policies creates more equity.	I didn't explain enough about the policies and how they relate to my thesis, especially the part about equity.	Expand section on policies; add more reasons why facts support my thesis.	Understood; look forward to revision. [a match]

In this taxonomy, there is an alignment between the instructor's written comments and Juanita's accurate perception of them. She constructed meaning fairly easily because her instructor was explicit in her written comments (and they would have appeared next to the section in the paper to which her instructor refers).

How Is This Taxonomy Useful in the Writing Classroom?

After posting comments or returning drafts with written comments, students select 4–6 major comments and record their perceptions (or misperceptions). Instructors can then comment in the far-right column: affirm, clarify, and/or redirect student. When students submit their final drafts, instructors can verify that students were or were not "good on their words" and implemented their plans for revisions. Last, instructors can tally the number of matches and mismatches of intentions and perceptions. Taxonomies encourage students to pay attention to their instructors' comments because they are held accountable to at least read comments and try to make sense of them.

Assignment #2: Write a literary analysis paper on a short story.

Table 6.2. Taxonomy of Instructor's Intentions and Students' Perceptions of Written Commentary for Assignment #2

Students	Instructor's Intentions	Instructor's Written Comments	Students' Perceptions	Match or Mismatch
Jasmine	"Expand your introduction to include more background information for an unfamiliar audience."	"What made you think that was enough background knowledge?"	"I was confused because I thought there was enough background knowledge, but I guess I need to add more."	Mismatch
Lori	"To help audience understand the concept of redlining."	"Explain why"	"I had already defined redlining, so didn't see a need to expand it."	Mismatch
Chris	"To add more analysis to support evidence."	"Not enough analysis here."	"I thought there was enough analysis, but I'll add more."	Match

Assignment #3: Write a short response paper to a reading.

Table 6.3. Taxonomy of Instructor's Intentions and Students' Perceptions of Written Commentary for Assignment #3

Students	Instructor's Intentions	Instructors' Written Comments	Students' Perceptions	Match or Mismatch
Luke	"To clarify speaker and addressee"	"Separate the name of the person addressed from the rest of the sentence."	"Fix punctuation error"	Mismatch
Keisha	"Change it [sentence] so that it reads smoothly"	"I asked her to talk about me with him, she asked him a few questions."	"Makes sense; make it understandable"	Match
Fatmina	"To keep tense consistent"	"have > has"	"Grammatical mistake; change to has"	Match
Cameron	"Clarify Point"	"Run-on"	"Fix run-on sentence"	Match

For both taxonomies (tables 6.2 and 6.3), several mismatches occurred between Mrs. Gates's intentions and students' perceptions. Why? Mrs. Gates's intentions are embedded too deeply or implicitly in the commentary, and students gave only cursory responses that revealed their lack of understanding. Unfortunately, the commentary did not achieve its intended goal of influencing students to improve their drafts in response to the rhetorical situation of the writing assignment.

Sometimes, students do not understand their instructors' written comments because they are implicit—often encompassing meta-language or subtext rather than explicit feedback. The subtext *is* the instructors' intentions, which do not always align with written comments as shown in the taxonomy. However, there were a few "matches" in which they aligned, which certainly lead to more focused, analytical papers.

When Mrs. Gates expressed her intentions explicitly, students tended to perceive her intentions accurately—and vice versa.

Overall, What Is the Key to Instructors Clarifying and Conveying Their Intentions?

The more explicit the comments, the more likely students perceive their intentions and are clear on necessary revisions.

SAMPLE SUMMATIVE COMMENTS ON BLOG POSTS

Summative comments are an example of holistic feedback that instructors provide at the end of papers.

Example Summary Comment

Your evidence points are logically sequenced and tied to the thesis clearly. Though you have some analysis points that interpret evidence adeptly, you can afford more to show your full understanding of [topic]. Your topic sentences are direct and support most parts of thesis; take a look at the second topic sentence; it's mismatched with _____. Introduction and documentation of quotes are solid. You've addressed my comments in these areas on the last paper. Keep this up! Main critique is that you have only a small number of credible sources, when more are needed to support your argument.

Return to the writing assignment to examine source requirements. (See section _____ of the course's writing handbook for more help with them.) Also, I'd like to see you use a more academic (rather than casual) vocabulary (e.g., "resulted in" rather than "ended up"). Plan for more revisions of a paper that has good potential. Addressing all these comments will help you meet your goal of raising audience awareness and fulfilling your analytical purpose. See my comments within your paper as well and contact me with any questions.

Example Summary Comment

In the first two pages of your argument, you skillfully use concrete details to support topic sentences. If you use the technique in class of highlighting evidence in one color and analysis in another, you'll see much less analysis. How can you interpret the evidence to answer why these details are important/relevant to the topic sentences/thesis? You set the audience's expectations about [topic]; therefore, prove your evidence for them. The upshot of your writing is improvement in topic sentences (not only topics, but answers to How? or Why?) since your last essay.

Likewise, selection and documentation of quotes. You've paid attention to my comments about sentence-level issues (e.g., commas and casual language), which resulted in higher audience awareness. In your next paper, I'd like to see more evidence of revision to make the argument fully convincing and fulfilling your analytical purpose. See my comments within your paper as well and contact me with any questions.

BLOG POSTS

The following postings demonstrate instructor's effective written commentary on students' writing that did not require revision.

Sample Draft of Hakeem's Posting

Assignment:

Who? Third-year college student, Hakeem
What? Short posting on prompt: Are Archetypes of Heroes and Heroines Socially Constructed?
When? Spring 2020
Where? Upper-level literature course at a New England college
Why? To demonstrate understanding of social construction theory as applied to literary texts (discussed in class)

Archetypes for heroes and heroines typically come from social values. The issue with social values is that they change. A stain on American society is how we viewed our Vietnam War veterans compared to other war veterans. American society glorifies the military. It preaches about the acts of bravery, valor, patriotism, and selflessness that the "heroes" in the military commit. From spitting on soldiers coming home from Vietnam who experienced brutal combat, to thanking a young soldier trying buy a meal at McDonalds who is "greener than grass".

Many of society's values have changed over time, but one that has remained is our admiration of athletic skill. From a Spartan Warrior competing in the Olympics of ancient Greece to Heisman winning quarterback Joe Burrow being picked first in the NFL Draft.

It is ingrained in society to be physically fit and to achieve athletic greatness. However, one sees even this ancient value trying to be changed by those who disagree with it. The "body positivity" movement is not only the opponent of this value, but a danger to society. Shaming fitness and trying to get society's values to change to theirs, even if their values would result in significantly shorter lifespans, massive spikes in health problems, and, as some U.S. Generals and Admirals would argue, a growing national security threat.

Instructor's Summative Comments

Note: Presented without marginal comments, because no revision was required.

Essay pivots between archetypes rooted in social values and archetypes reflective of changing social values. Managing both leaves the reader confused about your true point about values; consider one or the other to streamline posting. Also, contextualizing all examples (as you did with the Vietnam Era) would add clarity about roots of social values. Favorable examples of archetypes.

Your point about admiring athletic skill as an unchanging value contradicts your extended topic sentence, but follows with example of changing values about fitness archetypes. Clarifying purpose and direction of post, and ensuring that all evidence coheres around it would result in a solid explanation of archetypes and social values.

Noah's Posting

Assignment:

> *Who?* Third-year college student, Noah
> *What?* Short posting on prompt: Who Has Been a Hero in Your Life?
> *When?* Spring 2020
> *Where?* Upper-class literature course at a New England college
> *Why?* To demonstrate understanding of the hero concept as applied to the theme of the course: "Myths are Present in Our Everyday Lives"

When discussing heroes, *Star Wars* always comes to my mind, as it was one of my greatest influences as a child and is still to this day, especially when looked at through a more advanced lens. Specifically, the fate of Obi-Wan Kenobi in the original *Star Wars (A New Hope)* was always the definition of a hero to me, someone sacrificing their life for the sake of the betterment of society and/or the protection of others.

This was a character who was essentially "retired" and had no real stake in the galactic conflict at the time. He went from an overseer in the development of a young boy, to one of the largest actors in the eventual fall of the Death Star. Obi-Wan meets many of the previously discussed criteria.

First, he sacrifices his individual desires on countless occasions both as a Jedi before the fall of the Republic and as a mentor to Luke Skywalker. Secondly, he has an unmatched power and ally in the Force, allowing him to fulfill the role of a hero even further due to this power.

Thirdly and most importantly, he sacrifices his life immediately and without question or remorse upon realizing that Luke and his allies would attempt to save him and likely die as a result. A hero must be willing to go all the way in their quest, lukewarm fails to cut it, and the character of Obi-Wan Kenobi shows that aspect of a hero perfectly.

Instructor's Summative Comments

Favorable and clear topic sentence, tone, and focus. It is evident that you're a devoted *Star Wars* fan! Your unifying element of "sacrifice" plays out in various examples and seems convincing. Your point about Obi-Wan's power is isolated in that it does not fit your earlier criteria—stay consistent. Finally, your last point seems tacked on. Using a strong finish ensures that your audience takes away the significant point about the hero fulfilling all criteria. What else can you say about sacrifice and willingness to "go all the way"?

SAMPLE FORMATIVE AND SUMMATIVE WRITTEN COMMENTS ON ROUGH AND FINAL DRAFTS

The following rough and final drafts demonstrate the instructor's effective written commentary on students' writing that did require revision.

Peter's Sample Rough and Final Drafts With Written Comments

Who? Senior college student, Peter
What? Paper with prompt: What is the overarching message about the "Rashomon effect" (different perceptions of truth) as demonstrated in the film *The Usual Suspects*? What is the outcome of the "Rashomon effect"?
When? Spring 2020
Where? Upper-level literature course at a New England college
Why? To demonstrate comprehension of a concept about differing perceptions: "The Rashomon effect" as shown in a film; to connect the concept to the larger theme of the course: "Myths are Defined from Multiple Perspectives"

Peter's Rough Draft With Effective Written Comments

Note: Introduction and body paragraphs only.

The Usual Suspects **[KW1]**

[KW1: Create a title in your words/link to thesis.]

The 1995 crime drama, *The Usual Suspects*, is an exploration of deception and how far humans are capable of deceiving one another. The film focuses around themes of criminality, good vs. evil, loyalty (or lack thereof), and manipulation **[KW2]**. The film follows the narrator, Roger "Verbal" Kint, as he attempts to recount the events of the past few weeks.

[KW2: Four themes are a lot to tackle in a paper of this length. Which ones are the most prominent?]

Verbal details several of the heists that he and his fellow criminals executed that ultimately led to everyone in his gang, save for him, ending up dead during their final job on a boat.

The man responsible for his colleagues' deaths is shrouded in mystery and goes by the name of "Keyer Söze [KW3]." This [KW4] character illustrates the overarching point of The Usual Suspects: manipulation is a powerful weapon [KW5], one that is even more dangerous than bullying, coercion, or violence [KW6].

Manipulation is exercised throughout the film by the character Verbal, who is later revealed to be the criminal mastermind Keyser Söze. Verbal acts as the narrator of the film as he is being interrogated by Detective Dave Kujan [KW7]. Verbal quite literally delivers the narrative that he desires of the recent events that unfolded, all the while maintaining the composure of small, meek, timid man that lacks intelligence or a spine.

Since Verbal presents himself in this weak and insignificant manner, he is able to lull both the Detective and the audience into a complacency and acceptance of his narrative. This manipulation is exactly how Verbal (or Söze) is able to get away with killing his other four gang members, along with countless others along the way, and escape at the end of the film without consequences.

[KW3: Your summary that starts with "Verbal" Kint and ends with "Keyer Soze" is pitched just right as refresher for primary audience of educated adults who have viewed the film a few years ago.]

[KW4: No mention of "Rashomon Effect"/return to assignment.]

[KW5: Strongest part of thesis, but extend your thinking: Why do characters use manipulation as a means to reach their misguided goals?]

[KW6: "Bullying, coercion, or violence": adding three more topics moves in diff. direction/moving off topic.]

[KW7: Since Verbal is the mastermind, using active voice is more effective than using passive voice in putting agent in charge.]

Peter's Final Draft Excerpt

Note: Introduction and body paragraph only, with most comments addressed, shown within brackets [ ].

A Manipulative and Self-Interested Suspect

The 1995 crime drama, *The Usual Suspects*, is an exploration of deception and how far humans are capable of deceiving one another. The film focuses around themes of criminality, good vs. evil, and loyalty (or lack thereof). [Dropped "manipulation"] The film follows the narrator, Roger "Verbal" Kint, as he attempts to recount the events of the past few weeks. [Added: The account Verbal delivers contains several inconsistencies and holes which do not align with aspects of the one-going police investigation.]

[These inconsistencies represent what is known as the "Rashomon Effect," which is defined as "the subjectivity of perception on recollection, by which observers of an event are able to produce substantially different but equally plausible accounts of it" (*Psychology Wiki*).] [Added: In his recounting of the criminal activities] Verbal details several of the heists that he and his fellow criminals executed that ultimately led to everyone in his gang, save for him, ending up dead during their final job on a boat.

The man responsible for his colleagues' deaths is shrouded in mystery and goes by the name of "Keyer Söze." This character illustrates the overarching point of The Usual Suspects: manipulation is a powerful weapon [dropped "bullying, coercion, or violence"; added: used by those who are motivated by self-interest.]

[The Usual Suspects begins with an unassuming crippled man named Verbal Kint delivering his account of his criminal activity from the past few weeks to a detective by the name of Dave Kujan.] Verbal details how his gang of crinimals initially assembled after meeting one Manipulation is exercised throughout the film by the character Verbal, who is later revealed to be the criminal mastermind Keyser Söze.

What is notable about Peter's revisions? He narrowed his focus considerably in the second sentence and thesis, deepened his background of film as it related to his thesis, and rewrote the topic sentence to reflect active rather than passive voice for more directness—entirely appropriate because he was speaking of "manipulation." Peter addressed the majority of comments from the rough draft, which resulted in a substantial revision that focused mainly on content more than conventions.

Comments such as those provided for Peter's papers are considered "effective" for several reasons: they are specific, anchored near problematic areas, balanced with positive comments, and use a facilitative tone to ensure that Peter retains ownership of his writing.

CHAPTER 7

Audio Commentary

"Talking to students about their papers in person can be a remarkably efficient way to convey your thoughts about their work and be sure they understand what you've said, because you can speak more quickly than you can write, and because it provides your students with an immediate opportunity to ask you questions about your feedback, reducing the likelihood of misinterpretation."—"Giving Students Feedback on Their Writing," University of Michigan

BENEFITS OF AUDIO COMMENTARY

What Are Advantages to Using Audio Commentary?
Instructors have opportunities to express their comments verbally, which typically creates a greater understanding as students are used to classroom conversations and discussions—and audio commentary is an extension of these activities.

Why Should Instructors Consider Audio Commentary?
Instructors should consider audio commentary to

- create an exchange with student writers,
- move students from recipients to participants,
- create a dialogue in which they hear and respond to feedback in a similar way to an online or in-person conference,
- tailor comments to individual students, and
- manage the paper load differently and more efficiently.

What Is the Number One Objective of Students Listening to Audio Comments?

For papers requiring revisions, students want to know how to improve their drafts for revisions through an understanding of their instructors' comments. For final drafts, students want to gain insight into how and why their papers either met or fell short of expectations—and ways to improve their writing in subsequent writing assignments.

What Are Factors to Consider?

Factors to consider include length of time, template or framework, content, and tone.

Tips for tone are

- calm, steady voice quality
- volume within a moderate range
- deliberate, measured pace

What Role Does "Tone" Play in Conveying Comments Verbally?

Tone conveys acceptance, patience, and openness to students' strengths and challenges.

What Are Recommended Qualities of Tone—the Key Part of Audio Feedback?

Offer a direct, compassionate, or understanding, even matter-of-fact tone. Harsh, condescending tones can lose the message and render the comments ineffective (e.g., your thesis is ridiculous). Audio commentary seems to magnify difficult tones, which make students feel "called out" instead of engaged as writers and thinkers. The damage from tough comments is substantial.

What Are Examples of Comments That Convey an Accepting Tone?

- Tell me about . . .
- Would you share . . .
- I am interested in hearing more about . . .
- I'm curious about . . .
- OK, so you're saying . . .

- I am confused . . .
- You lost me here . . . help me understand . . .

What Are the Benefits of Audio Feedback?

Students are media-oriented and familiar with learning-management systems typically in place at schools. In addition, audio feedback

1. allows ease of access
2. is useful for a variety of writing assignments and assessments
3. is tailored to group projects or to individual students
4. allows for more in-depth detail
5. increases connection between students and instructors
6. removes overreliance on instructors; requires attention and participation
7. supports formative assessment
8. impacts feed forward
9. puts responsibility on students (e.g., to write down comments and engage in audio feedback as listening is required)

What Is a Useful Approach to Content of Audio Files?

Starting with a positive comment, move to a detailed analysis of the essay from beginning to end, constructive criticism on ways to improve drafts, and final summary comment.

STUDENTS' VIEWS OF AUDIO COMMENTARY

Based on surveys and informal conversations in the author's writing classes (freshman, junior, and senior college students), what are students' general perceptions of positives and negatives of audio feedback?

Positive

- Can pause/rewind to listen more than once
- Clearer
- Detailed; able to go more in-depth
- Different; "shakes things up"

- Easier to understand because perceptions are conveyed in certain tones
- Fewer misunderstandings
- Individualized
- Listen anywhere
- More informative
- More like conversations
- Praise seems louder

Negative

- Awkward—having to keep stopping to listen
- Fear of criticism that feels more "direct"; can be "put off" if there is a negative tone
- Have to write down comments
- Need visual of written comments; use with bulleted list of major concerns
- Technological issues
- Too much information/recommendations; pause more often to allow understanding
- Unable to ask questions

In survey after survey, these positives outweighed the negatives. The experience caught students' attention and guided them into constructive "conversations" about specific ways to improve their writing. The negatives are real and do require adjustments and patience with technology and training students to, in fact, write down the comments (not a bad thing) and engage more in the feedback process. Instructors could ask students to tape their own responses and ask questions as necessary. Then, true conversations will occur.

Based on surveys from college freshman composition classes in fall semesters 2018 and 2020, what are students' positive reactions to receiving audio commentary for the first time?

- "[I] really liked having the verbal commentary, because it was easier to comprehend what was expected for general revisions and places [to] focus on . . . felt like having a conversation with you."

AUDIO COMMENTARY 93

- "Comments were helpful and adding numbers to paragraphs helped to follow comments."
- "I didn't think I'd like it, but I actually do. I think hearing comments gives greater understanding of the emphasis of certain comments (better understanding of what is really intended) and make me feel less attacked than I sometimes do when reading feedback and feeling that my paper was misunderstood. It also gave me a point of reference to ask further questions."
- "I enjoyed feedback as it was better to hear it because the emotion and tone of comments was more clearly expressed."
- "I feel like audio commentary gives me much more constructive criticism so I can actually understand what I have done and how to improve."
- "I like the audio more than the written commentary. I comprehend better with the audio and the explanations seem more concise/clearer."
- "I much prefer this. I think it's a very valuable way to almost meet in person without having to accommodate schedules."
- "I was weirded out at first hearing your voice, but it was nice to be able to listen to it multiple times to try and see what I needed to improve."
- "It was more personable than writing comments."
- "It was very informative and I liked how it was given in the order of my essay was written (intro. → conclusion)."
- "New way. More like a conversation, helps very much to understand where the grader's perception/interpretation of my work is coming from."
- "The level of detail we depicted in our understanding of corrections proves audio feedback is successful in explaining to [us] what [our] strengths and weaknesses in writing are, and how to fix these."
- "Very good. I was glad it allowed me to hear it explained more than I have seen on paper in the past, and it allowed me to rewind to ensure I understand the comments made."
- "Very helpful. I ended up following along with the audio and writing your comments on my rough draft as if you had marked it up. This allowed me to better understand and target your comments."

Based on surveys from college freshman composition classes in fall semesters 2018 and 2020, what are students' negative reactions to receiving audio commentary for the first time?

- "[I] like having some sort of visual to look at while [I] revise."
- ". . . suggest to have both written and verbal feedback, because both have benefits, however, this may not be practical, as it would take too much time."
- "Everyone has a different learning style; audio may not be ideal for everyone."
- "First time; difficult [getting used to] first time."
- "Focus more on specific aspects of paper would help."
- "I like both; they both have their advantages and disadvantages. I like hearing the comments, but having written commentary means that I do not have to listen to the verbal commentary a dozen times."
- "Take slight pauses between different parts that would allow slightly more time to find that part of the paper and mark it for editing."
- "Tedious to rewind and listen to portion of feedback."
- "Use voicemail instead of Desire 2 Learn [learning management system]—we'll give you our phone numbers and not answer when you call."

For the most part, students are mindful that both written and audio ("the best of both worlds") would be ideal, but the time involved would be counterproductive given instructors' grading loads. If possible, then yes, a written list of bullets with major concerns is helpful, but audio commentary should include these same bullets at the beginning. Student engagement is key here, and for students to write comments (in Word files or in taxonomies) increases their understanding and ensures that they have listened to the audio feedback and, hopefully, will address it in revisions.

Based on author's surveys from college freshmen composition classes in fall semesters 2018 and 2020, how did students vote on preference for audio comments? Yes: 79%; No: 21%. With this in mind, what are tips to ensure a more successful experience with audio commentary?

- Ask students to number each paragraph or section, and refer to numbers when commenting.
- Avoid jumping around.
- Be direct, clear, and explicit.
- Be consistent across audio commentary segments—that is key; using a template supports fairness and reliability.
- Have a logical progression—either follow essay from beginning to end, or from major aspect to major aspect.
- Pause between sections to ensure that students have enough time to digest information.
- Read students' words/phrases/sentences when referring to them.
- Try to become used to the sound of your own voice.

Which Online Technology Supports Audio Commentary?

Voice memo on smart phone, *Garageband* on Mac, *SoundCloud*, and features on learning management systems (e.g., *Canvas, Blackboard,* and *Desire to Learn*) all support audio commentary.

What Is a Sample Template for Audio Commentary?

Start with strengths, compliment risks, and acknowledge effort (e.g., If I understand you correctly, you said ____, or I read that where you said ____, or It sounds as if you want to/or mean ____).

Aim to identify the student's

- intentions—what students seek to accomplish in their papers.
- emotions—which ones do students express in the papers about their subjects? Convey about the writing process?
- content—which 3–4 major issues of their papers do they need to address in revisions? (Think globally rather than locally about issues here.)
- recapitulate "recap"—how can students clarify their intentions, convey emotions productively in the process, address 3–4 major issues in revision?

Finally,

- explain how students can improve content in the next draft or writing assignment
- summarize your comments
- end with encouragement (e.g., taking these steps will make a more persuasive paper for your audience of _____)

TAXONOMIES

What Is an Example of a Taxonomy That Students Can Use While Listening to (and Reflecting on) Instructors' Audio Feedback?

This taxonomy supports a "check-in" to see if students understood their instructors' comments. Once taxonomies are returned, instructors can add their intentions behind the comments. The following taxonomies are from the author's doctoral research.

For Purposes of the Taxonomy, What Are Principles for Effectiveness?

- Instructors' comments are explicit rather than implicit for clarity.
- Instructors' written comments are broken down into singular points.
- Intentions are typically singular in expression.
- Students' perceptions tend to be reactionary (written without deep reflection), expressing one or several points.

In the following taxonomies, the instructor, Mrs. Gates, and her senior high school students in an advanced composition class participated in a case study for the author's doctoral research study on instructors' intentions and students' perceptions with respect to both written and audio commentary. Pseudonyms are used for all participants.

What Is the Method for Using This Taxonomy?

Students create a table with five columns. Label the first four Student's Name, Instructor's Comments, Students' Perceptions of Instructor's Comments, Plan for Revision.

Directions:

1. Write their names in column 1.
2. Make a list of 5–6 major comments on their papers in column 2.
3. Write their perceptions of comments—what they did or did not understand about the meaning in column 3.
4. Express their plans to address (or not, with explanation) comments in their revisions in column 4.
5. Return taxonomies to instructors—either hard copies or online; and instructors write "match" or "mismatch" in column 5.

Examples of Taxonomies for Student Use

What Is an Example of a Taxonomy That Students Can Use After Reading and Reflecting on Instructors' Audio Comments?

Table 7.1. Taxonomy of a Sample Assessment for Instructors' Intentions and Students' Perceptions of Audio Commentary for Assessment #1

Students	Instructor's Audio Comments	Students' Perceptions (What did you understand— or not— about the comments?)	Plans to Address (or Not/Explain) in Revisions	Instructor's Assessment	Matches and Mismatches of Intentions and Perceptions
Donovan	Extend thesis to answer "How?" or "Why?" to provide a clear position that Americans should notice where their clothes are made to help prevent child-labor abuses. A full thesis will give you plenty to work with and find evidence for.	Make my thesis longer to give me more to write about. Explain why Americans should pay attention to labor abuse.	Read more about child labor laws and rewrite the thesis.	Be sure to introduce the full thesis and look at the recommendation to do that. [Partial Match]	Match

Student completes this exercise.

For table 7.1, the assignment was to take a position and write a persuasive argument about a current controversial issue.

In this taxonomy, Donovan understood Mrs. Gates's intentions for him to revisit his thesis and answer the question: Why? Because Mrs. Gates made her intentions explicit and clear through her tone and expression, Donovan was able to discern her intended meaning quite easily. He plans to address her comments in his revision, which hopefully made his argument more focused and persuasive. Similar to other students presented in this chapter, there was a "match" between their instructor's intentions and their perceptions. Audio commentary contributed to this match significantly as it became an extension of the classroom dialogue, and students' understanding was notably greater.

What conclusions can we draw about Mrs. Gates's intentions and her students' perceptions? When Mrs. Gates made explicit statements during audio commentary—matching her intentions with her comments—her students generally perceived her intentions accurately. There was an alignment with two of three comments, which led students to better understand her comments and how to apply them in revisions.

For the mismatched comment, the student did not follow Mrs. Gates's thinking and sidestepped the real meaning of her point about word count. This could be remedied in a quick conversation between Mrs. Gates and her student.

For table 7.2, the assignment was to write a literary analysis of a short story.

Table 7.2. Taxonomy of Instructors' Intentions and Students' Perceptions of Written Commentary for Assignment #2

Students	Instructor's Major Comments	Students' Perceptions of Comments (What did they understand or misunderstand?)	Instructor's Intentions	Match or Mismatch of Perceptions and Intentions
Miguel	Realistically, the character Ian had to have done other things, or he has to set the record straight.	All right. I can change my paragraph to show a little more background on Ian.	He needs to make it more realistic.	Match
Kelly	Did they give you a word limit?	Mrs. Gates needs to know why information is compounded and a reason for lack of examples. Makes sense.	Her essay was too short. It's not well-supported, and it wasn't typical of the writing that she usually does.	Match

Students	Instructor's Major Comments	Students' Perceptions of Comments (What did they understand or misunderstand?)	Instructor's Intentions	Match or Mismatch of Perceptions and Intentions
Sakiya	A lack of correct grammar usually means that the vocabulary is not going to be high level.	I'm confused. Does Mrs. Gates want me to improve my grammar; then the vocabulary will improve, too?	Make the language believable and realistic.	Mismatch

Of the three scenarios, two matches and one mismatch occurred between Mrs. Gates's intentions and her students' perceptions. Why? For the two matched scenarios, Mrs. Gates was clear and explicit; for the mismatched scenario, her intention did not match her comment, leaving the student confused about the implicit comment. Written comments work best when they are explicit and match instructors' intentions.

For table 7.3, the assignment was to write a persuasive paper about a nonfiction piece of writing.

Table 7.3. Taxonomy of Instructors' Intentions and Students' Perceptions of Audio Commentary for Assignment #3

Students	Instructor's Audio Comments	Students' Perceptions (What did they understand or misunderstand about comments?)	Instructor's Intentions	Match or Mismatch
Yasmine	What made you come to that conclusion?	I don't understand the question because I don't know which conclusion she is talking about.	Include details so your conclusion is supported.	Mismatch
Anastasha	Explain why?	I now see the distance between characters and need to build in more dialogue and interaction between them so the audience can understand them and their conflict better.	To help the audience understand the relationship between characters	Match
Marco	Repetitious	I understand that I used the same words over and over and kept in some unnecessary info.	Eliminate unnecessary words.	Match
Abigail	I don't think your primary audience of high school students will relate to it very well unless you add some things to appeal to them.	The sentences and vocabulary are too simple—more for a young audience of middle-school students. I need to up the vocabulary.	Because she says her primary audience are her peers, write directly to them.	Match

Only one mismatch occurred between Mrs. Gates's intentions and students' perceptions. Why? Mrs. Gates's intentions are embedded too deeply or implicitly in the audio commentary, and students gave only cursory responses that did not reveal their full understanding. Three times "matches" occurred between Mrs. Gates's intentions and her student's perceptions, which is encouraging.

When Mrs. Gates expressed her intentions explicitly, students tended to perceive her intentions accurately—and vice versa. In her doctoral research, the author found more matches between intentions and perceptions when instructors delivered audio comments. In these instances, Mrs. Gates was more detailed and used a supportive tone to which students were accustomed.

How Is This Taxonomy Useful in the Writing Classroom?

After posting comments or returning drafts with written comments, students select 4–6 major comments, record their perceptions (or misperceptions), and express plans for revision. Instructors can then write their intentions. When submitting final drafts, instructors can verify (or not) that students were "good on their words" and implemented their plans for revisions. Taxonomies encourage students to pay attention to their instructors' comments and are held accountable to at least read comments and try to make sense of them.

Overall, What Is the Key to Instructors Clarifying and Conveying Their Intentions?

The more explicit the comments, the more likely students perceive their intentions and are clear on necessary revisions. Another common question regards approaches/frameworks/templates to delivering audio commentary. Some prefer a loose plan to follow to keep the experience conversational while referring to aspects of the writing assignment. Others prefer a more structured template to follow with all students. Either way, the key factors include being consistent, student-centered, and time-efficient.

The length of time for audio commentary sessions depends on the extent of the writing assignment: shorter essays take fewer minutes whereas longer essays take more minutes. Generally, five to ten minutes is adequate so as to not make the recording either too long or too short for impact.

AUDIOTAPED TEMPLATE AND SAMPLE

The following is a template for a research paper in a freshman college composition class.

Please have your paper on screen as a reference. I will provide comments using numbered paragraphs for clarity.

In terms of content, what did you do well? Preview.
In terms of content, what do you need to improve upon for revision of the paper? Preview.
Student and Title of Paper
Commendation(s) on Paper: Content
Recommendations on Content:

- Introduction
  - Thesis
- Assertions
- Evidence
- Analysis

Brief Summary

Case Study #1: Audio Commentary

Who? Freshman Gender Studies course/one student, Gabriella
What? Short Reflection Paper (assignment below)
When? Fall 2020
Where? Small college in New England
Which documents are present? Gabriella's rough draft, transcript of instructor's audio comments, Gabriella's final draft, analysis of impact of audio comments, and Gabriella's reflection on audio comments

Short Reflection Paper

Note: Full assignment in chapter 2.

Assignment: Write a response to one of the following prompts . . .

1. What is the state of feminism today? What have you observed that suggests where feminism lies in this "Fourth Wave: 2008–Present"?
2. What are stereotypes of men and/or women? Why are stereotypes true or untrue? What have you observed that supports your position?

Gabriella chose prompt #2.

Gabriella's Rough Draft

(444 words)

Gender Stereotypes: The 21st Century Plague

In the rising era of "Be True, Be You, Be Whatever and Whoever YOU Want to Be", gender stereotypes still plague the social construct of human beings. Woman are expected to be soft, gentle, and feminine, and are thought of as "weird" if they are not. In contrast, men are required to be strong, tough, and absent of emotion, and are ridiculed and known as a "sissy" if they lack these certain qualities that supposedly make a man, a man.

This is known as social construction or, "a socialization theory explaining the process whereby society structures these sex-linked categories and combines them with the commonly held perceptions about the accompanying psychological, physical, and behavioral attributes associated with the gender categories" (Lei 347).

Through middle school and high school, I was known as the "weird" one of my friends. While other girls braided their hair, painted their nails, went shopping, and talked about how cute that one boy in our psychology class was, I much preferred going to the firing range, watching football, and wanted nothing to do with the shopping mall. Now while this may have made me "weird", it is also what defined part of my identity. "Gender labeling results in forcing people to think in terms of polarities (either male/masculine or female/feminine) without accounting for individual differences not attributable to gender" (Lei 348).

Boys, on the other hand, are expected to be the opposite of females. This androcentric point of view is engrained into young boys' heads and is what shapes them to be the manly, tough, and absent of emotion individuals that many have become. In her article, Lei stresses that, "Gendering begins before the birth of a child . . . attributes of newborns such as 'strong,' 'robust,' or 'big' typically are perceived as masculine. Thus, they are socially construed descriptions for boys."

Yes, I believe these outdated stereotypes are still true, but it is due to social construction and introduction of these stereotypes at a young age that make these clichés present in our ever-progressive era of the "Be You" movement. These gender stereotypes are the prison bars keeping people from truly expressing themselves. By expecting a child to play with the Barbie doll you hand them or by ridiculing your friend who chose to join the cheer team instead of the football team, you are adding extra strength to these prison bars of limitations.

These constant expectations placed on young children all the way into adulthood shapes them to be someone they are not: merely the human form of a stereotype. Until we can look past these gender stereotypes, people will not be able to be who they truly want to be.

Transcript of Audio Comments for Freshman Student Gabriella

Note: Paragraph-by-paragraph approach.

1. Good afternoon, Gabriella, this is [instructor] here to comment on your Short Reflection Paper that you titled: "Gender Stereotypes: The 21st Century Plague." First, these are my content comments.
2. Stereotypes are a plague, which is a noun, but we can also think of it as a verb: stereotypes plaguing us unfairly so as you point out.
3. You seem passionate about the topic of gender equality, expressed as identity of "things decided for them."
4. I want to break down your paper through paragraphs with numbers. You have four of them, which I'll refer to as 1, 2, 3, 4.

5. In paragraph 1, your first line has a point (and I assume it's your thesis), but it's about self-expression outward, whereas your second sentence is about gender stereotypes plaguing social construct of human beings. There is a clash between them, so I recommend that you rebuild your thesis with your eye on your second-to-last sentence: "These constant expectations . . ." of paper. You discovered your thesis at end of the paper, which is not uncommon as writing is a process of discovery.
6. In paragraph 2, you did a good job with examples and quote selection, but it feels unfinished. What is at issue here? You indicated there are stereotypes plaguing and so forth, but what is at issue with people not being able to be who they are? This may be obvious, but catch this so you have a deeper essay to accommodate your audience.
7. Your example from childhood made me smile because you certainly pushed back on stereotypes and seemed confident in doing so. That's refreshing.
8. And, in the last part of paragraph 2, you have a quote about gender stereotyping, but it's not directly connected to your personal experience. Did you feel pressure from outside expectations—and pushing back on what was expected of you as a girl in the 21st century? How did expectations affect you?
9. That's one issue that I see overall is your quotes are not directly tied to your thesis and within paragraphs where they appear.
10. Moving on to paragraph 3, your focus on gendering begins before the birth of a child, which is a socially constructed theory; here's another opportunity to tie back to your "new and improved" thesis. Again, why is this at issue? What is the greater meaning here?
11. In the final paragraph, which is reflective, and does tie back to the "Be You" movement, you found your voice about gender stereotypes and the problematic aspect of them.
12. If there are so many problems with expectations, what is the result of this? A call for action at the end would work well.
13. This is the end of my content comments.
14. Now, I'll focus on conventions, which are sentence-level issues.

15. Comma goes inside the quote if no citation follows; found in line 1.
16. Think about vocabulary and shaking up a few words: these, this, and others that start too many sentences.
17. Overall, you have an above-average start here, Gabriella, and you have plenty more to say to kick it up a level so that it's a fully developed essay for your audience.
18. In summary, areas of focus include thesis, tying in and analyzing quotes, adding more details about impact on both yourself and others, and writing a strong finish.
19. This concludes my comments. Please e-mail any questions that you may have after listening to the audio.

Gabriella's Final Draft

(689 words—revisions shown in brackets)

Gender Stereotypes: The 21st Century Plague

In the rising era of "Be True, Be You, Be Whatever and Whoever YOU Want to Be," gender stereotypes continue to plague the social construct of human beings. Women are [constantly] expected to be soft, gentle, and feminine, and are thought of as ["unnatural"] if they are not. In contrast, men are required to be strong, tough, and absent of emotion, and are ridiculed and taunted as a "sissy" if they lack these certain qualities that supposedly make a man, a man.

This is caused by social construction or, "a socialization theory explaining the process whereby society structures these sex-linked categories and combines them with the commonly held perceptions about the accompanying psychological, physical, and behavioral attributes associated with the gender categories" (Lei 347). [Social construction, littered with gender stereotypes, limits a person from expressing their true identity and instead molds their identity into something it is not. When people feel that their identity clashes with these societal gender norms, they can feel as though they don't fit and belong among others.]

Through middle school and high school, I was known as the "weird" one of my friends. While other girls braided their hair, painted their nails, went shopping, and talked about how cute that one boy in our psychology class was, I much preferred going to the firing range, watching football, and wanted nothing to do with the shopping mall. Now while this may have made me "weird", it is also what defined part of my identity. [While yes, I definitely had my share of stereotype-driven comments, I was known as the kid that "marched to the beat of her own drum," and I rarely cared what anyone thought of me.

Many people I went to grade school with over the years, however, were not as fortunate to march to the beat of *their* own drum, and their feet frequently got stuck in the beat that society played all around them, trapping them from escape.] "Gender labeling results in forcing people to think in terms of polarities (either male/masculine or female/feminine) without accounting for individual differences not attributable to gender" (Lei 348). This incessant, unrelenting beat drowns out a child's beat, which can inhibit them from expressing genderqueer aspects of their identity.

Boys, on the other hand, are expected to be the opposite of females. This androcentric point of view is ingrained into young boys' heads and is what shapes them to be the manly, tough, and absent of emotion individuals that many have become. In her article, Lei stresses that, "Gendering begins before the birth of a child . . . attributes of newborns such as 'strong,' 'robust,' or 'big' typically are perceived as masculine. Thus, they are socially construed descriptions for boys." [How are boys expected to be anything but masculine when it is deep-rooted in their brains since birth that they must be?]

Gendering [at a very young age can ultimately lead to toxic masculinity, which not only has a harmful effect on men but on women as well. For our society to grow, people must be able to express who they are, not who they think they should be. This must start at birth, at the stop of gendering.]

Yes, I believe these outdated stereotypes are still true, and it is due to social construction and introduction of these stereotypes at a young age that make these clichés present in our ever-progressive era of the "Be You" movement. Gender stereotypes are the prison bars keeping people from truly expressing themselves. [By expecting a child to play with the Barbie doll handed to them or by ridiculing a boy who chose to join the cheer team instead of the football team, there is extra strength added to these prison bars.]

Constant expectations placed on young children all the way into adulthood shapes them to be someone they are not: merely the human form of a stereotype. Until we can look past these gender stereotypes, people will continue to struggle to be who they truly want to be.

Analysis of Impact of Audio Comments

Content

Addressed six of eight comments; 75%

Conventions

Addressed one of four comments; 25%

Comment about relocating her thesis was not addressed exactly, but it captured the spirit of the meaning and focused her thesis statement more acutely. She addressed: thesis, tied quotes to thesis, analyzed quotes, added more enriching details, and unified essay around unfair stereotypes (i.e., expectations of identity). She added one more vocabulary word, too.

Not addressed: call for action and thesis relocation.

Not addressed: comma inside quotes when no citation follows, introducing quotes, and citing quotes.

Overall, Gabriella addressed the majority of comments on content and addressed only a minimal amount of conventions comments.

Gabriella's Reflection on Audio Feedback

"I much preferred the audio comments to written comments for my writing. The audio comments allowed me to make out the tone of the person grading my writing, and better helped me to understand positive, negative, and neutral comments. Hearing my professor was much more personal than reading the comments off a rubric, although meeting about my writing in person would be even more personal.

"Meeting in person about my writing has its positives, but I often find myself forgetting what my instructor said from the five-minute meeting. Audio comments allow me to go back over the feedback as many times as I choose, and even listen to the feedback as I write. I listened to the comments all the way through once, then listened to them as I wrote by pausing as I fixed and corrected a certain part of my paper. Finally, I listened to my paper once after my paper was revised to ensure that I had corrected everything requested."

Case Study # 2: Audio Commentary

Who? One student, Jeremy, senior in high school
What? College Application Essay
When? Fall 2020
Where? High school in New York City
Which documents are present? Jeremy's rough draft, transcript of instructor's audio comments, Jeremy's final draft, analysis of impact of audio comments, and Jeremy's reflection on audio comments

College Application Essay

Prompt: Write a 400–500-word essay about climate change/the environment that has had a major effect on you and explain why.

Jeremy's Rough Draft

(504 words)

Ever since I was a child, I have loved to be out in nature. I loved to venture out in the void of our world, the unknown. I loved to see what the wild was truly like. My parents commented that when I was still a toddler, I was often scurrying out of their watch to see what was behind an alluring rock or what might lay beyond a particular tree. Since then, my love has never ceased, but grown. My deepest desire to be in the vastness of nature has never been stronger.

Any chance I get to venture out and see the wild, I jump at it skiing and hiking have fostered this passion, and without them, my love would be nonexistent

One particular aspect of nature that draws me in is being able to explore the natural, uncharted world. When I explore, I see a world free from the destruction of humans, free from the rapid industrialization and urbanization that has taken over our country I see a world abounding with new life where ecosystems survive completely on their own and animals outnumber humans two to one.

I see natural beauty unlike any other in the world. When I hike, I see jagged mountain peaks on top of each other, bigger than any sky scraper. I see waterfall stumble hundreds of feet. And I see rich rivers and lakes filled with aqua blue water flowing faster than a beating heart. When I ski, I see buttermilk snow encompassing miles of terrain as if you are floating in the clouds. I see snow packed trees that go on forever in the distance.

These sights give me the greatest satisfaction in life. I feel so blessed to be surrounded by the most beautiful sights in the world, and every time I am awestruck.

Nature also allows me to have an ease and sense of calm and comfort like nothing else in this world. When I am encompassed by my natural surroundings, I have not a care in the world. I am from free all anguish, anxiety, and challenges when I am exploring the uncharted. When I ski, I feel the silence of the snow, not a sound parades through my consciousness. When I hike, I feel the cleanliness of my breath and the fresh smell of greenery. If I am ever overwhelmed or worried, I think of the peace I get from nature, the serenity of life I can get nowhere else.

Nothing else in life has ever granted more satisfaction like no other place I have been comfortable than in the natural world. If I was notable to explore, or I didn't feel serenity when I am outside, I would not be the person I am today. Nature has taught me to respect life and respect the beautiful world we have been given. These values reinforce my morality even when they are virtually non-existent everywhere else, and I vow to protect this very thing that gives me life.

Transcript of Audio Comments for Freshman Student Jeremy

Note: Paragraph-by-paragraph approach, starts with overall assessment.

Good afternoon, Jeremy, this is [instructor] here to comment on your College Application Essay. You have mainly addressed the prompt and used enough detailed description to engage the audience; you also created a sense of movement and flow that matches actions of skiing and hiking. I appreciated your passion, too. First, these are my content comments:

1. The introductory paragraph is very choppy and needs to flow better and introduce your points clearer; add commentary about family after the first paragraph.
2. In paragraph 1, the sentence "Any chance I get to venture out . . . non-existent" is repetitive from your other essays. Try to vary your ideas because the same admissions people will read all of them.
3. You're missing a clear thesis that relates to the prompt. It may be buried with the hiking and skiing comment; make it more prominent in revision.
4. In paragraph 2, the sentence with ". . . rapid industrialization and urbanization" veers away from the prompt, which you should stay loyal to.
5. At the end of paragraph 3, you use great imagery; think about adding descriptions of exploration and the meaning it gives to you.
6. Toward the end of paragraph 4, the sentence "If I am ever overwhelmed or worried, I think of the peace I get from nature, the serenity of life I can get nowhere else" trails off and, overall, makes an unclear point.
7. In paragraph 5, this sentence "Nothing else in life has ever granted more satisfaction like no other place I have been comfortable than in the natural world" seems too philosophical and is repetitive. How is this experience unique to you?
8. At the end of paragraph 5, you again become too philosophical; focus concretely on the unique outcome of nature for your final paragraph. Create a strong finish for your primary audience.

These are my conventions comments:

1. In paragraph 1, the sentence ending with word "grown": is this word necessary for the primary audience to understand? If so, clarify.
2. In paragraph 3, use first-person to stay consistent throughout the essay; sentence ". . . encompassing miles of terrain as if *you* . . ."
3. In beginning of paragraph 4, you switch the order of skiing and hiking—stay consistent in sequence.

In summary, you have a good foundation but need to avoid mixing voices (yours and authority's). There are a few bumps with words/phrases that all detract from the meaning. See what you can do in revision to create overall consistency in noted areas.

Jeremy's Final Draft

(486 words—revisions shown in brackets)

Ever since I was a child, I have loved to be outside in nature. I loved to venture out in the void of our world, the unknown. I loved to see what the wild was truly like. [Skiing and hiking have fostered this passion, and they allow me to explore and give me a serenity I can find nowhere else.]—*moved to make thesis more prominent.*

My parents commented that when I was still a toddler, I was often scurrying out of their watch to see what was behind an alluring rock or what might lay beyond a particular tree. Since then, my love has never ceased, but grown. My deepest desire to be in the vastness of nature has never been stronger. Any chance I get to venture out and see the wild, I jump at.

One particular aspect of nature I love is exploring the natural, uncharted world. When I explore, I see a world abounding with life where ecosystems survive completely on their own and animals outnumber humans two to one.

I see natural beauty like any other in the world. When I hike on these explorations, I see jagged mountain peaks on top of each other bigger than any skyscraper. I see waterfalls tumble hundreds of feet. And I see rich rivers and lakes filled with aqua blue water flowing faster than a beating heart.

When I ski on these explorations, I see a sea of buttermilk snow encompassing miles of terrain as if you are floating in the clouds. I see snow packed trees that go on forever in the distance.

These sights give me the greatest satisfaction in life. I feel truly blessed to be surrounded by the most beautiful sights in the world, and every time I am awestruck.

Nature also allows me to have a sense of calm and comfort like no else in the world.

When I am encompassed by my natural surroundings, I have no care in the world. I am free from all anguish, anxiety, and challenges when I am exploring the uncharted. When I hike in nature, I feel the clean in my breath and the fresh smell of greenery. When I ski in nature, I feel the silence of the snow, not a sound parades through my consciousness.

If I ever am overwhelmed, or worried, I often think of the peace and clarity of mind I get from nature, the serenity of life I can get nowhere else.

[This exploration and peace of mind combine to form a unique outcome in me. They have shaped my identity more than anything else, they have taught me to live my life with respect for others and for nature. This has allowed me to have more meaningful relationships and strengthen my respect for the exploration and the serenity nature offers. Without this, I would not be the person that I am today, and for this reason, I value nature above all else.]

Analysis of Impact of Audio Comments

Content

Addressed six of eight comments; 75%

Conventions

Addressed one of three comments; 33.3%

In summary, Jeremy addressed the comment about thesis (relocated and made more prominent), keeping his voice consistent and authentic, varied some ideas for primary audience, and deleted all comments that were repetitive and philosophical. He replaced the entire paragraph at the end with a more concrete description of how nature is unique to him. He did address two comments: improving flow in the introductory paragraph and, at the end of paragraph 4, about the "unclear comment." Jeremy addressed only one convention: he switched the order of skiing and hiking in paragraph 3, but he did not change the pronoun "you" to "I" or replace the vague word "grown" in paragraph 1.

Overall, Jeremy addressed most of the content comments and relatively few convention comments. His final draft was stronger in voice, focus, and answering "why" nature is unique to him. He could use one more draft to fully address comments, but that is his choice.

Jeremy's Reflection on Audio Feedback

"I think verbal comments take it to another level, but written comments are more limited. Teachers can elaborate more in verbal comments and explain things more in-depth. Written comments are good to go back over and see what you missed, too."

FINAL CONCLUSION ABOUT AUDIO COMMENTARY

Audio commentary proves to be a useful and unique approach to commentary that engages students to pay more attention and participate more fully in the feedback process.

CHAPTER 8

Emotional Component

> "Asymmetrical power relations in the assessment process risk involving negative emotions, which may form a barrier to learning from feedback. One person's helpful suggestion may be another person's judgmental criticism."—David Carless, "Differing Perceptions in the Feedback Process," 229

As instructors, we have all experienced students' emotional reactions to receiving feedback: elated to anger and every emotion in between. Students perceive comments through the prism of their experiences. There are students who sing our praises and those who speak to us (or about us) indignantly with perceived injustices of unfair criticism and/or lower grades than expected. There are students who put halos on our heads because their expectations were met, and students who "melt down" in front of us because their expectations were not met.

Students' reactions tend to be extreme on both ends of the spectrum, whereas the middle group remains more impassive. Still, student emotions play a paramount role in the feedback process, which is why an entire chapter is devoted to this domain. The emotional component of feedback has not been addressed enough in the research, yet emotions remain a highly influential part of students' reactions and actions of their writing, which bears analyzing to find ways to manage emotions in the feedback process.

EMOTIONS IN THE AFFECTIVE DOMAIN

In Educational Terms, Where Do Students' Emotions Have a Place in the Feedback Process?

Emotions play a role in the affective or expressive domain that accompanies every act of writing. In this domain, students express emotions, and instructors help students (and themselves) to identify and regulate these emotions.

What Role Do Students' and Instructors' Emotional Investments Play in the Feedback Process?

Commenting on student papers: these four words raise a myriad of emotions in instructors, from disgruntled to relieved to hopeful. Instructors may dread returning papers knowing that some students will react with anger, disappointment, or both. However, they may look forward to returning papers if enough students receive higher grades. Instructors' and students' emotions play a major part in the feedback process in writing classrooms, in the affective domain with their investment in writing assignments.

Instructors make an emotional investment in students through their instruction, curriculum, and commentary. Students make an emotional investment in assignments and want returns on their investments (sometimes very specific ones) with fair comments and grades. Unlike assignments in algebra and biology, student writing takes a different sort of investment in which criticism feels sharper than a math comment telling them a formula is wrong or that a lab report needs better sequencing.

Regarding investments in writing, sometimes they are realized, sometimes not. One way to address this disconnect is for instructors to take the time to address emotions either 1:1 or in class discussion to ensure that feedback "lands" where it should in the student writing development chain. If instructors and students express their emotions in a productive manner—within a day or two of returning papers—more benefits accrue then and in the future. A shorter time frame to address emotions regarding papers is most impactful. Otherwise, the process is muted and becomes similar to chewing gum without the flavor.

EMOTIONAL COMPONENT OF THE FEEDBACK PROCESS

What Is the "Emotional Component" of the Feedback Process?

Because writing is ultimately a personal, vulnerable process with an emotional component built in, this process needs attention to enhance ways students receive feedback. Students' emotional responses affect their perceptions; likewise, instructors' emotions affect their intentions. Students may see low grades and tough comments as personal attacks on them rather than their performance. Instructors may see low grades and honest comments not as attacks but as accurate evaluations of student performance. Both have specific expectations that do not always align.

Students do need constructive criticism as instructors consider a balanced approach using strategies, such as facilitative comments, in this text. In the process of disclosing their thoughts and emotions as well as position on topics, students take risks. To ensure that they are nurturing writers, instructors support risks and "have their students' backs" while both holding them accountable and helping them process their feelings around comments and grades. The emotional goal of feedback emphasizes the need to open up rather than shut down learning to keep instructors sane and energized, and to keep students motivated.

What Is Inherent in the Feedback Process That Evokes Emotions?

The asymmetrical instructor/student relationship can result in conflict in which emotions are caught in a negative cycle. The emotions include defensiveness versus upset, impatience versus confusion, demanding versus disappointment. They may disagree on who "owns" the student's writing and ways to improve the writing process. Instructors and students have different perceptions of accuracy and fairness as noted by their opposite, yet surprisingly similar emotions, which can cause miscommunication. Though they may have an easy rapport in the classroom, the tone changes in the feedback process when instructors become judge and jury, and students become defendants.

This hierarchy naturally causes conflict unless both instructors and students engage to achieve writing goals. Other challenges inherent in the feedback process involve students not operating at a functional level of understanding their instructors' commenting vocabulary and ways to implement it as well as having to adapt to different instructors' commenting styles. Both challenges warrant addressing in the feedback process. Within this hierarchy, students' emotions affect their thinking processes greatly; either they feel distracted from reflecting on written feedback, causing their writing development to be impeded; or they accept feedback in the spirit in which it was intended and grow as writers.

With more engagement on both sides, the imbalance can lessen and result in greater impact on positive ways students perceive themselves as writers and the writing process.

What Are Common Emotions of Instructors as They Comment on Papers?

Return to the stages of grief: denial, anger, bargaining, depression, and acceptance. In opposition, they may feel joy, relief, satisfaction, excitement, and contentment if student papers meet or exceed their expectations. Generally, most instructors would agree that they enjoy seeing the application of their instruction in students' papers but prefer having graded rather than grading.

What Aspects of Instructors' Delivery Carry Emotional Weight?

These emotions include carefully choosing tone and diction, which students may interpret accurately or inaccurately. Written commentary, on papers or online, carries more opportunities for misinterpretation, whereas audio commentary carries fewer misinterpretations because students can detect their instructors' tone and match it with their spoken words. This act mimics the classroom dialogue, which is highly familiar to them; therefore, audio comments become an extended part of this conversation.

What Is at Issue With the Emotional Component of the Feedback Process?

If feedback is a one-way process in which instructors provide feedback with the assumption that students will comprehend their comments fully, then typically students' misunderstandings and negative emotional responses occur. On the other hand, if feedback is a two-way approach with instructors providing feedback, and both instructors and students have opportunities to express their intentions and perception (e.g., in discussions about taxonomies in chapters 6 and 7), students' understanding and more positive responses occur.

What Do Instructors and Students Experience During the Feedback Process?

Instructors want students to read, digest, address, and transport comments across papers. Instructors may feel frustrated if students do not address enough of their comments in revisions, though encouraged to do so. On the other hand, students sometimes see the process as one sided and view feedback as compartmentalized and nontransferable from paper to paper. They want more fair, understandable commentary that provides clarity on ways to improve their drafts. Instructors may feel that their commentary is, in fact, clear and understandable, yet students feel frustrated if they perceive commentary otherwise. Instructors want students to pay attention to both content and convention comments, then apply all comments in revisions.

Students sometimes just want to see grades and ignore comments, or to apply only the comments they see as valuable for a revision, rather than all of the comments that instructors deem necessary. Students may want more comments on content rather than conventions, which is not realistic if enough sentence-level issues exist to distract from meaning for audiences. (Good writing and commentary practices suggest waiting until the editing phase to comment on sentence-level issues, not focus solely or predominantly on them.) Clearly, there are mismatched intentions and perceptions in their communication about writing. Essentially, both sides want to be heard and understood.

To this end, classroom discussion prior to due dates of papers about commentary practices and associated emotions is an important step in managing expectations. (The Emotional Vocabulary List on page 132 is useful for these conversations.) Both sides can express their emotions in a safe space, thus allowing for authentic expression and potential solutions.

For instance, instructors can ask students what strategy to use when their emotions are running high when receiving feedback and grades. What can they do to "cool off" and still receive constructive criticism adequately? How can the trust factor remain in place even with constructive criticism? These discussions are often enlightening and help to temper emotions after returning papers because students (and instructors) now have different approaches to express them in more productive ways.

What Role Does Trust Play in the Feedback Process?

When instructors and students have a professional relationship built on mutual respect and trust, feedback is less likely to trigger negative responses. The less instructors know their students, the wider the distance between instructors' intentions and perceptions; consequently, feedback is more likely to prompt positive responses. For instructors, helping students to identify and express their emotions can enhance the feedback process by using cognitive empathy and active listening (and teaching students to express the same), key ingredients to building trust.

Also, students need reminders of the trust factor, even when receiving constructive criticism, to do their part to engage in the process to better understand how to receive negative but well-intentioned comments.

What Does Research Suggest About Connection of Emotions and the Feedback Process?

In a study by Brackett and colleagues from Yale's Center for Emotional Intelligence, a sample of instructors divided into group "A," which wrote an essay about a "good" day; and group B, which wrote an essay about a "bad" day. Once finished, all instructors graded a student's essay (the same one for both groups). Results showed that "instructors who wrote about a 'bad' day prior to scoring the essay, on average, issued a whole letter grade lower than instructors who wrote about a 'good' day prior to scoring the student's essay."

The results showed a direct correlation of instructors' moods with grade levels of student performance on essays. According to Brackett, "When we are unaware of our feelings, we're likely to be biased (positively or negatively) based on how we're feeling . . . it's important to check in with ourselves and be aware of our feelings. When we do that, our feelings are less likely to bias our thinking" ("Feelings Influence Decisions"). So, what does this mean for commenting practices?

Prior to the feedback process, it is important that instructors check in with their moods and adjust them when necessary to manage their biases toward students' writing. Awareness is utmost in this process. Because students "read" their instructors' behavior on a regular basis, they are keenly aware of instructors' moods when reading their comments, which immediately influences their own opinions as well as sharpens their perceptions positively or negatively. When commenting on students' papers, especially as the pile grows larger, instructors can use reset buttons to manage moods, noticing how they are influencing their comments and grades.

Other reset buttons include taking breaks, resequencing papers to be fair to both ends of the alphabet, using grade-norming sessions with colleagues, and sample papers/rubrics to keep instructors on more objective tracks. Instructors are human, of course, but they still need to strive for as much objectivity as possible, especially on bad days.

STUDENTS' EMOTIONAL REACTIONS TO FEEDBACK

What Is a Continuum of Students' Rich and Varied Responses?

Angry	Disagreeable	Indifferent	Agreeable	Elated
Very Sensitive	Sensitive	Under-sensitive	Less Sensitive	Not Sensitive

Figure 8.1. Continuum of Students' Emotions. *Author created*

To use this continuum tool effectively, instructors ask students to identify their emotions before and after meetings about their papers, which assist them with awareness of emotions that may have dominated their thinking.

What Are Various Student Reactions Based on Triggers?

Triggers create a dissonance between the feedback and learning processes; here are several types of triggers that create this dissonance:

- Truth triggers: Honest assessments of student writing that are challenging to hear or see; students react along the lines of "don't make me face myself and my flaws as a writer."

- Relationship triggers: Comments that activate feelings about relationships between instructors and students; all commentary lives within relationships; in other words, comments are not exclusive from relationships.
- Identity triggers: Comments that prompt students to react as writers—past and present. These triggers reveal their "baggage" from past writing-based courses in which they received positive or, more often, negative comments, which stay with them as developing writers. These comments tell a story about who the student "is" as a writer and prompt future emotional reactions that may interfere with the feedback process.

When meeting with students about feedback, instructors can share these triggers with them, asking students to identify each one and how it applies to them and their papers. Students can also share their continuum tool, expressing their emotions before and after meetings. This results in labeling emotions in each scenario for clarity and collecting more information to help students cope with feedback more effectively.

What Are Three Typical Reactions to Feedback That Students Perceive as Unfair, Unjust, Inaccurate, and/or Unhelpful?

1. Blame instructors' teaching and commenting styles: They believe that they have followed the assignment, perhaps met 1:1 with instructors (or writing tutors), and revised to standards, yet grades are lower and comments more negative than expected.

   How to shift students' blaming behavior? Validate their feelings. Have a conversation about how they (or both sides) may have contributed to the outcome and ways they can adjust their behavior for subsequent writing. If warranted, instructors may verify style and further explain motives to students.
2. Doom and gloom: They believe they "screwed up," did not meet their own or instructors' expectations, and criticize themselves.

   How to shift students' self-critical behavior? Validate their feelings. Have a conversation about realistic performance and ways to diminish negative thoughts to see feedback as "actual size," rather than outsized. Set goals for subsequent writing.

3. Disappointment that manifests as anger and fear: They believe they have disappointed their instructors, then turn to anger at the injustice of low performance as not their fault. They could also feel disappointed in themselves, which also turns to anger expressed outward because it is challenging for students to face their fears.

How to shift students' negative emotions? Validate their feelings. Have a conversation about why the student earned that grade and ask about their understanding of feedback. Set goals for subsequent writing.

What Are Several Scenarios of Students' Misperceptions of Their Instructors' Comments?

- After continuously writing "vague" on a series of drafts, a colleague's eighth-grade student approached her at the end of the school year, asking confusedly, "What does 'va-goo' mean?"
- A freshman college student received feedback on his paper that included the acronym "PV." When asked to interpret the acronym, he said "proverbs" and "post-victory." He did not know that "PV" stood for passive voice. When asked the meaning of passive voice, he said he did know what it meant.
- After returning rhetorical-analysis papers, a colleague's first-year college student approached him and said, "You said I needed to put forth more effort. Why didn't I get a higher grade? I tried hard on this paper."

What Is the Cost of Students Misreading Feedback—and a Solution?

The cost of students mishearing or misreading comments is high. It results in wasted opportunities after the time-consuming, thoughtful process of providing commentary. How can instructors manage students' emotions? Students select 3–4 instructor comments and add them to column 1, they express their understanding of comments in column 2, and then instructor completes column 3. This exercise creates opportunities to identify and clarify students' perceptions in relation to instructors' intentions of comments. The results often show the distance between their intentions and perceptions, yet create opportunities to balance them in the future and to determine mismatches to address before the next writing activity.

They also prompt a class discussion about the overall findings of the exercise with students providing their own examples aloud. Though this exercise includes only 3–4 major instructor comments, they can yield plenty of useful data. The table consists of instructors' comments, students' perceptions of comments, plans to address (or not) in revision, and designation of "match" or "mismatch."

Overall, the goal is to disassemble distortions in students' thinking so they can truly understand the results of their performance and ways to do better on the next round.

INSTRUCTORS' EMOTIONS RELATED TO FEEDBACK

What Are Common Instructors' Emotions When Plagiarism Is Present in Student Papers?

Suspected plagiarism always raises instructors' emotions: anger, disappointment, and frustration. They may even feel a sense of betrayal after spending quality time in class discussing documentation of sources. A typical instructor response is to lash out at students, sometimes before collecting all the facts (e.g., Why did you plagiarize? What is wrong with you as a writer? After all we discussed in class about documenting sources, how could you do this?). Conversely, students may feel attacked, diminished, and angry—even if they did, in fact, plagiarize. To mitigate these situations, the recommendation is to meet 1:1 with the student (and a witness if needed) to ask such questions:

- What process did you use to locate sources?
- What do you understand about citing sources?
- What is your understanding of paraphrasing (often the most likely place plagiarism occurs)?
- Did you notice any concerns about the research process as you were locating sources and writing?
- What is "plagiarism," and why does it occur?
- Did you approach documenting sources honestly?

Next, instructors share their concerns and present facts from both sources and papers. They then ask students to explain the situation and proceed from there. (Whether students are honest or dishonest requires different steps at different institutions.) If plagiarism occurs, instructors need to express their truthful emotions and concerns about students becoming credible researchers and allow students to do the same.

This continues to build trust, even in difficult emotional situations. If absent, this is a missed "teachable" moment to show students the role emotions play in these tricky scenarios. Lastly, instructors can stress that these are isolated incidents, express the seriousness of the issue, administer punishment as necessary, and encourage students to do better on future papers.

What Are Unhelpful Approaches to Managing Emotional Components That Stall the Writing Development Process?

These include habitual strategies: writing very few comments; giving only grades without comments; using harsh criticism/personal attacks; delaying returning papers significantly; marking every error; and, overall, taking ownership of students' writing. Comments based negatively in emotion will not help students to grow as writers who see themselves as "owners" of their writing.

Difference Between Constructive and Destructive Comments, Encouragement and Reprimanding Comments

Constructive comments that identify skill gaps and explain how to fill gaps empower students to address feedback in their revisions or future papers; destructive comments that are attacking or dismissive result in students thinking, "the instructor didn't like my paper because he didn't agree with my position on ____."

Encouraging comments promote better esteem in student writers because they appreciate praise that is genuine and not overdone. Positive comments result in students thinking, *How can I improve my writing?* and boost their perception of themselves as writers. For instance, Jeremy, a college freshman, said, "It's good to know what I got right." On the other hand, reprimanding comments prompt students' self-protection and avoidance of responsibility; they feel reduced and do not perceive their instructor's good intentions to help them grow as writers while "having their backs."

It is also important to look at the other side when students may confess, or instructors may elicit confessions about "little to no effort" or "rush jobs" on papers. Instructors may elicit the truth with a simple statement to students: "Fess up," then cope with the honest or dishonest fallout. If handled with expressed emotions, this can result in favorable events in which students grow as writers. Constructive criticism is necessary but is best received when conveyed with fairness and hope that students can do better next time.

What about praise? These comments fall on a continuum with "barren" on one end and a "compliment fest" on the other. The recommendation is to fall in the middle of the continuum.

Here are a few recommendations about praising students' writing. Basically, praise the process, not the students personally. They do not trust too much praise that seems disingenuous. Research shows that too much does not improve their self-esteem as writers. Students want to know how they can improve—even if they receive high grades on papers—and accept a balanced number of praiseworthy comments.

Examples of overly praising students' writing personally:

- "You performed wonderfully with no errors, Kathleen."
- "Your writing is the best in the class; I wish other students would take your lead, Lucia."
- "Your writing is ready for publication, Marcus."
- "You're the only writer in the class who produces awesome work, Louisa."

Examples of balanced praising of students' writing:

- "You must have worked really hard on this paper!"
- "I see you chose to add _____, which makes a more developed point that will be welcomed by your audience."
- "Wow—it looks like you really enjoyed that project!"

These types of comments allow students to evaluate themselves, rather than receiving their instructors' evaluation passively. This results in a disconnect from their writing. However, more facilitative approaches with praise can spark students' curiosity and exploration in furthering the writing process.

Examples

- Praise what students can control—
  (e.g., "You combined those sentences, which makes your point more understandable.")
- Focus on descriptive feedback, rather than too much praise—
  (e.g., "You created better logical progression in this paragraph, which is now easier for your audience to follow.")
  (e.g., "I noticed that you switched topics. Tell me about your decision-making process.")

EMOTIONAL INTELLIGENCE (EI) AND COMMENTARY

What Is a Working Definition of "Emotional Intelligence"?

Mayer & Salovey (1997) define emotional intelligence as "The ability to monitor one's own and others' feelings, to discriminate among them, and to use this information to guide one's thinking and action." The assumption here is that emotions influence thinking, metacognition, and behavior.

What Are Emotional Intelligent Approaches to Managing Students' Immediate Emotional Reactions to Their Unmet Expectations About Feedback and Grades (as shown in textbox 8.1)?

- Assess the instructor's own feelings of concern, fear, anger, frustration, and other negative (or positive) emotions relative to commenting and returning papers. Push the reset button and present a professional response.
- Assess students' various negative (and/or positive) emotions before proceeding with a 1:1 conference. Plan ways to address their emotions with strategies in this chapter.

- Avoid squelching opportunities for teachable moments when students' emotions thwart their rational thinking. Address their emotions; otherwise, they are likely to "grow louder," which may taint writing development. After all, "emotions largely determine our actions" (Brackett 2019, 31).
- Call for a twenty-four-hour cooling-off period before meeting to discuss papers. (If necessary, diffuse immediately by "checking in" with students' emotional states.)
- For virtual classroom conferences, beware of hitting the "send" button too quickly without a self-assessment of comments. Ensure that they are not destructive or too reprimanding, balanced with constructive and encouraging comments.

What Does a Reasonable Feedback Process After Returning Papers Look Like?

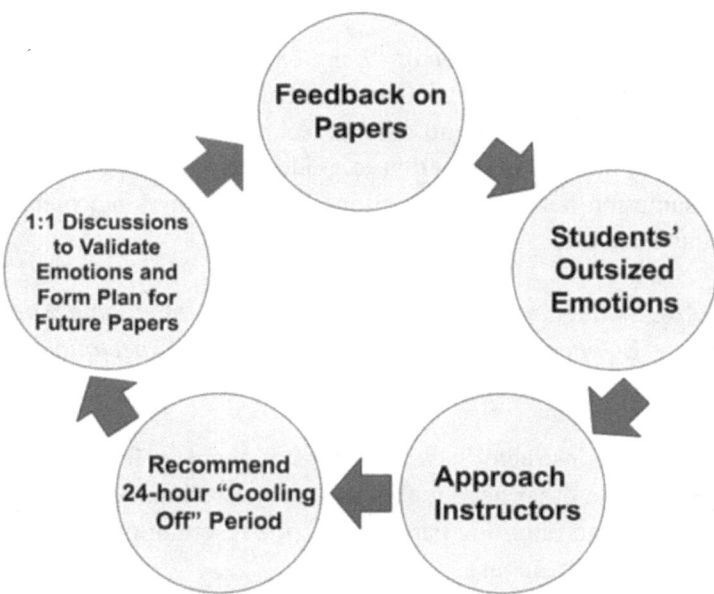

Figure 8.2. The Feedback Process After Returning Papers.
Author created

What Is a Useful Approach Using Emotional Intelligence to Provide Feedback That Helps Both Students and Instructors Better Manage Their Emotions During the Feedback Process?

Instructors can . . .

- ask students to identify emotions (Emotional Vocabulary List) (see page 132)
- balance encouragement and constructive criticism
- be "emotional scientists" rather than "emotional judges" (Brackett 61), which means becoming a commenter through inquiry and observations rather than only criticisms. In other words, respond rather than react (see figure 8.3)
- realize that "emotions are data" (Brackett 2019, 17), and emotion manifests itself in behavior. Assess both instructor's and students' emotions before proceeding with 1:1 conferences about comments
- set emotional goals for the revising process and giving/receiving feedback
- use audio or online written commentary so that students have the context of comments and can better detect tone. All of this serves as data for them to better perceive instructors' intentions more clearly

What Are Further Approaches to Managing Students' Emotional Reactions in a 1:1 Conference or Brief Discussion as Promoted in This Text?

- Address performance based on learning objectives—tie all comments to them.
- Continue to get to know students to build trust and enhance communication.
- Focus on students' performance ("just the facts") rather than their motives, which always evokes defensive reactions.
- Help students to increase accurate self-assessment using strategies.
- Introduce your stance as an "audience of one" (acting as a reader and responder, rather than a grading machine).
- Promote co-regulation: mutual or two-way communication with the end goal of students learning to regulate their own emotions.

- Tailor feedback with clear guidance on how to improve sentence-, paragraph-, and essay-level gaps.

What Questions/Statements Can Instructors Direct to Students in the Midst of Strong Emotional Reactions or Later in Draft Conferences?

- How do you see the situation differently than expressed in my comments?
- I have some concerns and feel optimistic that we can overcome them.
- I may know how you feel about _____, which is similar to my own experience in a high-school or college class when I received _____.
- I perceive that your emotions are based on _____.
- It is entirely appropriate to feel _____ on reading feedback.
- What are your chief concerns that we can address together?
- What can I do to help you accomplish your goals in revision or the next writing assignment?
- When you submit papers late or ask for unnecessary extensions, I feel _____.
- Why do you feel the way you do about my feedback?

AUP: ASSESS, UNDERSTAND, AND PLAN APPROACH

What Is a Useful Approach to Managing Instructors' and Students' Reactions to Feedback?

The AUP approach as in textbox 8.1 and figure 8.3.

TEXTBOX 8.1.
The AUP method

Assess: Quickly assess your own emotions, as well as your students' emotions, briefly validating them. Seek questions from students about feedback. Plan a meeting afterward to provide enough time for both instructors and students to read and reflect on the feedback.

Understand: Meet with students on a one-on-one basis and ask them to label and express their emotions about the feedback (Emotional Vocabulary List). Express your own feelings. Find common ground to understand the intentions and perceptions of the feedback. Ask questions and clarify.

Plan: Advise students on regulating emotions effectively to achieve writing goals. Form a plan for future writing assignments and communication about emotional component. Ask students to use taxonomies, editing journals, and/or other methods (chapter 6) to log comments and apply them to the next writing.

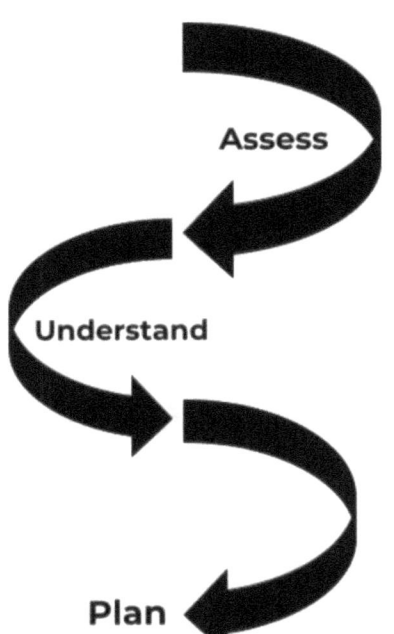

Figure 8.3. The AUP Method Graphic.
Author created

Why Do Students Not Address Our Feedback?

This is explained in more detail in chapter 5, but here are more emotion-based reasons:

- Emotional responses (e.g., anger and frustration) block understanding and application.
- Internal radar keeps things safe—they stay in their comfort zone.
- Past negative experiences of feedback influence their perceptions.
- Students scan for what is wrong, not right; they feel discouraged by setbacks.
- Students see writing courses as a necessary rather than useful experience in their education.
- Students are self-immunized against criticism; they have learned to minimize its impact or compartmentalize negative feedback.

EMOTIONAL VOCABULARY LIST

The emotional vocabulary list is a useful tool for students to identify their emotions toward the feedback process and use in discussions with instructors:

> Positive emotions: assured, cheerful, confident, content, determined, elated, encouraged, enthusiastic, excited, fulfilled, glad, grateful, gratified, happy, hopeful, joyful, optimistic, passionate, pleased, proud, relieved, respected, satisfied, secure, uplifted, and valued
> Negative emotions: angry, annoyed, anxious, depressed, disheartened, passive, resistant, sad, somber, uninspired

APPLICATION OF EMOTIONAL INTELLIGENCE APPROACHES IN THE WRITING CLASSROOM

Scenarios Reflecting Emotional Intelligence in the Classroom

Mrs. Natalia Duncan, a retired high school English instructor in Ohio, explains how she manages the emotional component, including building trust, with two students:

Scenario 1

I consider myself a writing tutor. My busiest season occurs between August and the end of the calendar year as students start their college application essays. This year I was fortunate to work with an exceptional young lady as she approached her senior year. Savannah and her mom met me at the local restaurant. Upon seeing them together, it was easy to see that Savannah was adopted. Mom went away to order food and Savannah some beverages as Savannah and I looked over her "Common Application Essay" with 500-word limit. Before we could get very far, Mom returned and emphasized that Savannah was not her sister who wrote easily and clearly.

Savannah struggled, according to her mother. Granted, this writer showed up with 1,200 words, an autobiography. The rewarding aspect of working with Savannah was two-pronged, a love of music (she played six instruments) and her passion for anything STEM. We just had to cull from her experiences the story of how she had developed her two high school families, band and the robotics team. Savannah diplomatically suggested that Mom explore some stores while we got down to work. I always stress that the essay is the writer's, not mine. I ask permission to write ideas and suggestions on the hard copy of the essay.

I also always express my gratitude that the writer is trusting me with her essay because writing is a personal endeavor. I sincerely complimented Savannah on the rich résumé that her essay communicated, and then I asked if she could select one incident from band and one from her robotics team experience that are vital to an admissions officer knowing who she is. The entire time we worked she made intelligent choices, questioned my suggestions, and wholeheartedly participated in her revision.

Approximately two hours later, any reader could understand Savannah's growth as a band and orchestra member. Drumline is her musical family complete with teamwork, friendships, nicknames, and inside jokes. A once shy Chinese girl recognized the links between the rules and rhythms of music with its eventual improvisations. These similar laws of math and science translate into robotic theories, designs, constructions, innovations, and competitions. I suggested that Savannah conclude her essay with the realization that her adopted family encouraged activities that helped her find the two "families" that nurtured her passions. Being honest, Savannah did not incorporate my suggestion for her conclusion, but after all, this essay is her essay. She trusted me. I know this because she invited me to two band halftime shows; one took place at the high school from which I retired.

Scenario 2

Trends in education come and go, but research validates the importance of an instructor's relationship with each student. Language arts education helps establish trust through reading, writing, and discussion. This rapport is essential for meaningful and healthy growth as a result of self-reflection. For example, my classroom website opens with, "My goal is to see what each student needs and help meet those needs." I have witnessed many examples that support this goal.

My last ten years in the classroom are full of stories validating the emotional component vital to working successfully with teenagers. Short incidents outside the classroom affirm my belief. Opening the high school's writing clinic at 7 a.m., I often greeted the few early risers who crossed my path, usually on their way to the weight room. Some were first in line outside the writing clinic ready to conference. One dark winter morning my "Good Morning" and "How are you?" were answered with a very flat and unbelievable, "OK."

I did not have this young man in class, but as we sat on a chilly window ledge in a deserted hallway, he shared that his father had just been put on an organ donor list. He talked. I listened. That's what he needed. I don't remember if he ended up in my speech class or in one of my AP Language and Composition sections, but I do remember that this brief encounter established a rapport, a level of trust, that transferred positively to his classwork.

One memory in particular stands out in my mind. One tall, lanky redhead was going to drop AP Language and Composition. He stayed after class, crying and feeling overwhelmed. He could not meet the deadline for our *Great Gatsby* unit final essay. As a result of our superintendent's opening day address, I had paired this novel with excerpts from Paul Tough's *How Children Succeed: Grit, Curiosity, and the Power of Character* and Carolyn Dweck's *Mindset: The New Psychology of Success*. Students were to analyze a character as he or she relates to these readings. Noah's one-week deadline extension yielded not only a sophisticated character analysis, but also an honest, self-actualized conclusion. (And, let's be honest, I could not possibly respond to all 65 essays in anything less than one week.) Noah chose to embrace Tough's emphasis on developing grit in the face of a challenge.

Noah also admitted that he, a work in progress, wanted to identify, not with Dweck's fixed mind-set, but with the author's growth mind-set. Trusting in his week's extension and in his epiphany helped Noah to thrive in AP Language and Composition, to lead boys' volleyball from a club to a varsity sport, and to apply his emerging philosophy to a successful college career. I trusted Noah not to take advantage of me with this extension, and he trusted me to treat him fairly.

As shown in these two scenarios, trust is the key element of emotional intelligence in the writing and feedback processes. Without trust, resentment festers and stalls student writing development. Emotional intelligence, as applied to the feedback process, calls for instructors acting as emotional scientists rather than judges, examining their own emotions, and, likewise, allowing students the opportunities to have "emotional moments" after receiving feedback—and processing them together.

In addition, setting forth a reflection period in which students reread comments, then return to calmer minds in meetings, proves beneficial. Fostering students' growth as writers produces a greater mutual understanding of commentary. In other words, meaningful encounters in which students' emotions are acknowledged as natural, even expected, parts of reactions and reflection will produce more matches between instructors' intentions and students' perceptions.

CHAPTER 9

Feedback on Feedback

"Reflecting is providing feedback for yourself."—Patty McGee, *Feedback That Moves Writers Forward: How to Escape Correcting Mode to Transform Student Writing*, 207

SELF-REGULATION OF FEEDBACK

What Is Meant by "Providing Feedback for Yourself"?

Providing feedback for yourself includes several components: Instructors examining their own feedback as well as students examining their own writing and providing feedback to themselves, which essentially means that they explain their writing to themselves and use any insights in revisions.

What Are Two Parts to the "Self-Regulation" of Feedback?

The two parts are, first, students' cognitive skills to process meaning of feedback to achieve objectives of writing assignments; and second, students' metacognitive skills to actively observe and monitor (regulate) their cognitive processes. In other words, "self-regulation" refers to aspects of students' thinking, motivation, and behavior during learning processes, guided by their writing goals—both individual and collective—for papers.

What Is "Co-Regulation" of Feedback?

Co-regulation is a mutual partnership between students and instructors to negotiate the meaning of feedback in hopes of lessening distance between their intentions and perceptions—all to improve students' writing development. Students are proactive, rather than reactive, which means they assume ownership of their writing.

At Which Three Levels Do Students Internalize Instructors' Feedback?
Cognition, motivation, and emotion.

What Inhibits "Self-Regulation"?
Feedback that is difficult to understand and requires students to supply too much of the meaning inhibits self-regulation. Productive feedback helps students regulate their emotions and thinking processes, whereas unproductive feedback causes dysregulation of these same processes.

TEACHING METHODS TO INCREASE STUDENTS' SELF-REGULATION SKILLS

Which Teaching Methods Increase Students' Self-Regulation Skills?

- Ask students to identify strengths and needs in their own writing—look back at various comments on writing assignments; track comments in taxonomies; use editing logs.
- Create a writing assignment whose sole purpose is to reflect on instructors' commentary and ways students did or did not address comments (and why); use the results to set a plan for future papers.
- Create assessment workshops in which students and instructors develop rubrics or other assessment tools together.
- Create carefully constructed rubrics that tie in emotional intelligence.
- Lead discussions about rubric criteria and expectations of assignments in class near the time of introducing the assignment.
- Seek students' feedback on feedback about rubrics after its use for papers. Which criteria were clear? Which unclear?
- Use rubrics in students' peer reviews.

How Can Students Become More Self-Regulated Learners?

One example is a survey students complete to accompany drafts. They reflect on the rhetorical situation of the paper using their metacognitive skills. The result? More intention by student writers who raise the rhetorical awareness in their writing. Surveys such as the two that follow encourage students' self-regulation of the writing and peer review processes.

SURVEYS

Survey 1: Rhetorical Situation and Content

- What is my purpose in writing this argument? Have I fulfilled my purpose?
- Who is my primary audience? Have I convinced them of my position?
- Have I used appropriate vocabulary for my primary audience?
- Have I clearly explained my thesis (message)?
- Have I contextualized my writing (explained background as appropriate for my primary audience)?
- Have I used my peers' reviews in my revisions about content?

Survey 2: Conventions

- What sentence-level issues have I addressed?
- What problems did I notice on my editing log (chapter 10)?
- Have I corrected typos and spelling errors?
- How have I used my peers' reviews in my revisions about sentence-level issues?

Survey 3: Self-Regulation (Reflection)

- How have I used writing as a tool for learning?
- What have I learned about myself as a writer?
- To what extent did I reach the objectives of the assignment?
- How I improved my sentences since the rough draft?

APPROACHES TO FEEDBACK ON FEEDBACK

What Are Ways to Discourage Co-Regulation of Feedback?

- Too many directive comments equals low self-assessment and low co-regulation.
- Instructor's purposes replace students' purposes.

What Are Ways to Engage Students in the Feedback Process?
Students . . .

- are encouraged to see their writing as a whole, rather than many parts that instructors comment on
- ask questions on drafts; instructors respond only to those questions
- decide which drafts to grade (e.g., three of five writing assignments)
- e-mail a "troubled" paragraph or section of drafts to the instructor who, in turn, provides written or verbal feedback on the paragraph with the intention that the student will apply the advice to the remainder of drafts (e.g., what are the three things that would make a difference in my draft?)
- respond to immediate opportunities for reflective exercises and taxonomies—once they have listened to audio comments, or have received papers with written comments—either handwritten or online
- take the "Feedback-on-Feedback Survey"
- use sticky notes on subsequent drafts with students answering the question: How did you use feedback from previous draft(s)?

The main goal of self-regulation activities related to feedback is for students to come to know that they are responsible to respond and act upon the feedback to grow as writers.

What Are Ways to Encourage Students to Take Risks in Their Revisions?

- Rewrite 2–3 paragraphs or even 2–3 sentences.
- Create an outline of a longer paper after rather than before completion, which can reveal a need to resequence and/or reshape paragraphs and sentences.

Once in Place, What Does Students' Self-Regulation Look Like?
Self-regulation

- considers and uses suitable feedback
- makes an effort in different phases of writing process
- employs metacognitive skills—reflects on feedback and adjusts goals as needed
- is open to developing as an academic writer
- provides positive and constructive criticism in "feedback on feedback" opportunities
- revises writing
- seeks further feedback

CHAPTER 10

Feed Forward

"Good feedback is a powerful element in learning. Ultimately, however, the impact feedback has on learning depends on how the learner responds to feedback."—Pirjo Pollari, "To Feed Back or to Feed Forward?" 11

What Is "Feed Forward" in the Feedback Process?
For purposes of this text, feed forward relates to

- students reflecting on their instructors' feedback
- instructors reflecting on their feedback method
- instructors reflecting on their students' responses to their own feedback

All are important to gain insight into the impact and meaning of commentary. Ideally, students should see instructors' comments as "portable" draft to draft so that they are meaningfully interconnected across a school term.

Both informal and formal feedback methods are used in the classroom. Informal methods include conversations and responses, and formal methods include student interviews, reflections, and surveys, and methods to inform instruction.

FEED FORWARD IN THE CLASSROOM

What Does Feed Forward Look Like in the Classroom?

Engagement with feedback looks like students actively involved in monitoring their own performance. Feed forward also looks like instructors using students' responses to their feedback to inform instruction. For instance, instructors can show lists of major communication matches and mismatches—relative to commentary—which they then use to set goals with the class for the next writing assignment.

BENEFITS OF FEED FORWARD

What Is the Benefit of Feed-Forward Approaches?

Repositioning feedback as feed forward invites students to engage in the process proactively while focusing on improvements in their writing. The focus on feedback in feed forward opportunities is all the "selves": self-regulation, self-directed learning, self-efficacy, and self-advocacy.

What Does "Feed Forward" With "Co-Regulation" Look Like in the Classroom?

Here is the pattern: Students write within a process, instructors provide helpful feedback during the process (formative assessments), students provide feedback (responses) to their instructor's feedback, and instructors use their feedback to inform instruction and commenting practices. In other words, feed forward uses a full feedback loop in which students and their instructors are engaged together to improve writing.

What Is a Three-Fold Method to "Feed Forward"?

1. Instructors provide opportunities for students to address or act upon feedback in revisions or subsequent writing assignments.
2. Instructors hold students accountable (or foster a sense of obligation) for reading and addressing comments using taxonomies, editing logs (see below), or other methods.
3. Instructors seek students' feedback on their feedback to inform instruction.

EDITING LOG

Example of an Editing Log (as designed by instructors)

In future papers, I plan to use

_____ transition words between paragraphs (e.g., however, moreover, accordingly)
_____ commas in compound sentences (e.g., Dr. Martin Luther King Jr. spoke on civil rights, and he made a profound impact on all audiences.)
_____ commas after introductory phrases at beginning of sentences (e.g., During the Civil Rights Era, protests were common.)
_____ academic words, not casual ones: ended up, talks about, and first off (e.g., resulted in, discusses, first)
_____ no commas in MLA citations (Jones 6).
_____ the author's last name and page numbers in citations—for example (King 9).

IMPACTS OF FEED FORWARD ON INSTRUCTION AND LEARNING

What Impacts Feed Forward?

- Aligning language of the classroom, writing assignments, rubrics, and commentary.
- Requiring students to summarize major comments and write revision plans to address comments in papers.
- Asking students to provide feedback on instructors' feedback and rubrics.
- Asking students to explain which types of comments are useful and not useful. (Because this is not a typical event in the writing classroom, students genuinely appreciate the chance to provide their own feedback, which is another example of students participating in the feed forward process.)

Examples of students' negative comments include "Too many questions," "Too many harsh comments/feel 'called out' often,"

"I'm not always clear how to improve my writing from your comments," and "I cannot read your comments very well."

Examples of students' positive comments include "Thanks for relevant comments," "Audio comments are different and made me pay attention," and "Detailed comments helped me to know what is important, and typed comments online were easier to read."

- Returning papers as soon as possible after submissions has greater impact on understanding and applying commentary.

Feedback-on-Feedback Survey for Students (designed by instructors)

- Which types of comments are useful? Why?
- Are there types of comments that are less useful or any type of comments less usual? If "yes," why? Even though you may have perceived them as "less useful," did you address any of them in your revision (or next writing assignment)? If "yes," explain how.
- Did you address useful comments in your revision (or next writing assignment)? If "yes," to what extent? How did you address useful comments in your revision (or next writing assignment)? (e.g., extended thesis to answer "Why?")
- Overall, why did you or did you not address comments in revision (or the next writing assignment)?

How Does Students' Feedback on Feedback Relate to Instruction?

Students' feedback—what they understand and misunderstand (as reported in taxonomies from chapters 6 and 7)—can shape and streamline commentary, discard comments that cause negativity, or keep comments that positively impact on revision. Reading survey results can make instructors eat humble pie, but at least they know whether or not their comments are working. Better use of time and greater impact on revisions are beneficial.

How Can Survey Results Inform Instruction?

Surveying students about their perceptions of feedback (What do they understand? Not understand? What did the instructor not understand?)

adds greater insight into the process. Similar to the example in chapter 8 about a student's misreading of "vague" comment to "va-goo," instructors learn of students' misperceptions and have chances to correct them. Survey information, such as perceptions of audio versus written comments, yields valuable information that can support methods of commentary that have the greatest impact on revisions or subsequent assignments. Finally, results can help time and energy efficiency of the feedback process.

How Can Students' Commentary Inform Instruction?
Students' commentary

- prompts collaboration on rubrics
- influences approaches to paper load (as discussed later in this chapter)
- prompts discussions about writing, assignments, and performance
- guides instructors to rework lessons to create space/time to discuss their approach to feedback
- shapes peer reviews that address commentary in different ways
- streamlines commentary; prompts instructors to discard non-useful types of comments

Students are more likely to address comments if they are engaged in the feedback process, because then students are participants, rather than recipients, which helps "buy-in" of the process.

What Role Does Transfer Play in the Feedback Process?
Transfer draws on, reworks, and creates knowledge by using

- comments as bridges from assignment to assignment
- knowledge of the writing process, rhetoric, genre, discourse community, and content
- a completed metacognitive exercise on feedback: What can I take to the next paper? Which comments are "portable"?
- editing logs, taxonomies, and surveys to transfer knowledge across papers

MANAGING FEEDBACK WITH LARGE CLASS SIZES

What Are Ways to Reexamine Feedback in Light of Large Class Sizes With Multiple Papers?

Sometimes grading papers seems like an unmanageable workload that is simply overwhelming. One goal of this text is to offer many suggestions and alternatives that instructors can use to adapt to their own situations.

Figure 10.1. The Comic Strip. *Jonny Jimison*

What Are Reasonable Approaches to Manage the "Paper Load" (NCTE)?

This text should not end without acknowledging the significant challenge for instructors to provide feedback for multiple sections with large class sizes and many papers. The following are recommendations for managing the feedback process:

- Ask students to write a "mini" version of their rough paper using only index cards (an exercise in conciseness), then comment only on the cards.
- Comment on 1–2 page(s), then ask students to use the feedback as a guide to correct errors on subsequent pages.
- Commit to no more than 2–3 hours outside of class on particular days to provide comments.
- Distinguish between treatable and untreatable areas, and focus on treatable areas.
- Draw a line when a paper loses traction; stop commenting and ask the student to address the commented areas.
- Focus on major rather than minor areas; move out of the "censor in chief" role and focus on major, rather than minor, issues.
- Give completion grades for effort toward the writing assignment.

- Instead of a variety of comments, ask only a series of questions that students then address in their revised drafts (and indicate where they answered them).
- Instead of marking the same errors across papers, use a "common faulty areas" document for class—focus on patterns (audiotape this list, too).
- Lean on peer reviews—pairs or small groups—to decipher comments; make lists.
- Post partial rough drafts (using a larger font) in the classroom, and ask each group of students to rotate through to comment on given sections (e.g., introductory paragraphs, thesis, and/or evidence paragraph) for the writer to address in revision.
- Select only two papers from a portfolio of five papers to comment on; students choose the two papers.
- Use a "Twitter" approach, and write a summary comment using no more than 280 characters.
- Use audio comments.
- Use more formative rather than summative assessments.
- Use the motto "less is more"—fewer well-developed comments rather than longer series of them.

To summarize commenting practices:

- Diagnose major issues.
- Write a few (3–4) well-developed comments that align with diagnosis and how students can improve areas.
- Prioritize areas in need of improvement.
- Act as a representative reader or "audience of one."
- Focus on students' intentions.
- Adapt comments to writing process.

OVERALL CONCLUSIONS FROM THIS TEXT

- The feedback process flourishes when instructors and students develop a trusting relationship with open communication.

- Comments can have tremendous impact if instructors convey their value and hold students accountable for not only reading but applying them in subsequent papers.
- Students pay attention more to content than convention comments; they need training to focus on sentence-level issues with exercises.
- Various strategies presented in the text are ways to make the feedback process more efficient and effective.
- Feedback strategies can lessen distance between instructors' intentions and students' perceptions of commentary.
- Feedback can inform instruction and future commenting practices using a feed forward method.

GUIDING QUESTIONS OF THE TEXT

Returning to the Guiding Questions of This Text, How Would You Answer Them Now?

1. How can the feedback process become more effective for student writing development and less burdensome for instructors?
2. How can we engage students more in the feedback process to achieve greater gains in their writing development?
3. Why do instructors and students have such different expectations of feedback? How can the sizable gap between instructors' intentions and students' perceptions lessen to impact writing development?

Through feedback practices, instructors can help students gain confidence in their own abilities as thinkers, writers, and readers.

APPENDIX A

Terms of the Feedback Process

affective qualities: Emotional expression verbally and nonverbally

assessment: Descriptive feedback on process of student learning; identifies strengths and needs

bi-directionality: Two-way communication

cognitive skills: Thinking skills to process content to achieve learning objectives

diagnostic role: Identifies gaps in students' comprehension and expression of knowledge

dialogic writing: Writing with reciprocal responses; in this text, instructor and students

dissonance: Mismatch between instructors' intentions and students' perceptions; incongruence between facts and beliefs

evaluation: Using numbers or letters, judgment on basis of criteria about the product of student learning

exigence: "Imperfection marked by urgency; it is a defect, an obstacle, something waiting to be done, a thing which is other than it should be . . . in any rhetorical situation there will be at least one controlling exigence which functions as the organizing principle; it specifies the audience to be addressed and the change to be effected" (Bitzer 1968, 6)

feed forward: Students addressing instructors' commentary across drafts; instructors examining patterns in their commentary and student performance to inform instruction

feedback: Content + effectiveness; commentary on student's performance—verbal, written; unspoken and spoken

formative assessment: Descriptive feedback during process of learning that students apply in their writing
interlinear comments: Instructors' written feedback within students' paragraphs; it is anchored near problematic and praiseworthy areas
metacognition: Thinking about thinking; monitoring one's own thinking processes
references:
- **criterion-referenced:** Compares students' work to criteria
- **norm-referenced:** Compares students' work with entire class
- **self-referenced:** Compares students' writing to their past writing performance

rhetoric: Writing designed with audience, purpose, message, and context in mind
rubrics: Criteria for students' writing with consistent descriptors for each level of performance so that students can demonstrate the specific learning objectives
sociocultural: Constructed meaning or understanding of cultures within a social context
stylistic choices: Sentence variety, conciseness, emphasis
summative assessment: Descriptive feedback after process of learning
terminal commentary: Instructors' commentary on students' products with assumption that revision will not take place
types of knowledge:
- **declarative:** Knowing "that"
- **procedural:** Knowing "how?"
- **schematic:** Knowing "why?"
- **strategic:** Knowing "when, where, and how"; application of other three types of knowledge

webfolios: Online publishing featuring students' writing—sometimes with multiple drafts of given papers

APPENDIX B

Case Study of Formative and Summative Online Comments for Half- and Final Drafts of Research Paper, Freshman English Composition Course

BACKGROUND: PROVIDING ONLINE FEEDBACK

Given current circumstances, providing online (digital), rather than written comments, can be more efficient. It is not always realistic to handwrite comments on every paper with the challenge of students not reading cursive handwriting, which leads to more of a necessity of online comments in a virtual classroom.

One effective approach to providing online comments is to create "stock" or common comments for an "A" paper, "B" paper, and so forth to an "F" paper. Instructors create a Word document of common comments (or use feature on learning management systems) such as praise, questions, and constructive criticism. (See chapter 5 on "Commenting Vocabulary" for examples.) An example of a common comment is "Thesis is difficult to follow," then, tailor it for each student, rather than write a separate bank of comments individually.

In the following series of drafts for Alexander, a freshman in an English composition course, several online steps are reflected in these documents:

- Half-draft is due approximately halfway through a six-week research-paper process.
- Instructor's stock comments: content and conventions on half-draft—individualized to Alexander.
- Final draft is due at the end of the six-week research-paper process.
- Instructor's individualized and common comments tailored to Alexander.

Each step is designed to convey the value of comments and the need to address them in subsequent revisions and to transfer across writing assignments. Each step holds students accountable for comments rather than students dismissing them or viewing them as compartmentalized for each assignment. It is unlikely students will address all their instructors' comments—usually 70%, as doctoral research in this text suggests, but this approach still puts the spotlight on the need to pay attention to feedback in the writing development process.

CASE STUDY

Who? Alexander, college freshman
What? Research paper on a social justice issue; 3–4 pages with 3–4 sources; interview and counterargument not required at this stage
When? Spring 2021
Where? Freshman English composition course at small New England College
Prompt: Take a position on a social justice issue in America and write a persuasive argument. Direct your argument to a primary audience.
Note: Instructor was the author of this text.
Documents Present:

- Alexander's half-draft of research paper
- Instructor's formative written online assessment of half-draft
- Alexander's final draft of research paper with revisions addressing commentary
- Instructor's summative written online assessment of final draft of research paper
- Alexander's reflection on instructor's online comments

Alexander's Half-Draft of Research Paper

Lingua Franca: Speaking American

Improper grammar at times? Maybe. Unique pronunciation? Quite possibly. In your lifetime, you have likely had numerous interactions with people who speak English as a second language or with those trying their best to learn it. As anyone who has taken a beginner foreign language class much traveling to a foreign country where a different language is spoken know, speaking a non-native language is extremely difficult. Yes, improper grammar with its unique pronunciation tends to be characteristics of second language speakers' speech.

It's is perfectly acceptable and understandable. But how do these characteristics affect perceptions on non-native speakers? As research suggests, English language learners with foreign accents, often perceived unfairly as "broken English," are subject to negative bias leaning to linguistic discrimination. This stigma around their language ability marginalizes them socially and places disadvantages on career and educational advancement opportunities.

The language rooted in a wide spectrum of views ranging from xenophobic sentiments to subconscious bias, nonetheless, no matter where the bias lies on the spectrum, its discriminatory effects are unacceptable. Of course, as others may argue, English language learners should strive to master their language ability in order to succeed in America. In any case, people need to be accepted; let's not marginalize English language learners and make it hard on them. These problems can be tackled head on as American society recognizes these language biases and seeks to fully accept English language learners. Americans must endeavor to eliminate language discrimination and accent bias by acknowledging the issue, seeking a greater understanding of differing cultures and linguistics, advocating for progressive qualities that help English language learners, and ultimately embracing English language learners' place in American society.

As the most widely used language globally, English is often referred to as the universal business language. The demand for English speakers is, in fact, has created a large disparity between the number of native and non-native speakers. In an estimation, "roughly 70%" of more than a billion English speakers worldwide are not primary language speakers, but rather learned it as a second language (*Ethnologue*). Looking into American demographics, in 2018, there was a reported "44.8 million foreign immigrants living in the United States" (Budimann). With these staggering statistics in mind, it only makes sense that there are numerous variations of the language distinct from what some would consider standard "American English".

Differing accents and speaking mannerisms seems most natural coming from such a diverse population of English speakers, not to mention learners. While they rarely admit it as much, American Native English-speakers often take for granted that their native tongue is so widely spoken. When attempting to communicate with others, English is often a safe bet. This fact, however, has led many Americans to become comfortable in the belief that "English is the standard" and has created unfair expectations for immigrants and foreigners in their English abilities.

The ease of communication through English has numbed monolinguistic native English speakers to the world beyond. Rather than lending an ear in and seeking to understand others, many choose to keep walls of separation between their connections to others. Language barriers exist, but they can be deconstructed. In more extreme cases, those who hold intolerant opinions such as "This is America, speak English!" or "Learn proper English!" end up building language barriers even higher. As it has been said repeatedly before, America is a melting pot. Ideally, diversity should be accepted. Language and culture identity should be accepted. Yet, xenophobic, and bigoted sentiments harm the melting pot. All citizens, whether native-born or naturalized immigrants must be accepted. All visitors to our country, regardless of origin and language, must be accepted. It would be counterintuitive for a diverse country like the United States, which does not have an official language, to reject or discriminate those who speak language outside of English.

Of course, English is the lingua franca (common language) which allows ease of communication throughout the country. Just like any other language, English connects us to each other, helping us understand one another, speak to opinions, tell stories, and conduct business. Thus, the ability to speak English and speak well should be strived for in America. Nonetheless, accents, differing speaking mannerisms, and even "broken English" should not be stigmatized or cause for linguistic discrimination. There is no such thing as "speaking American'; language is unique to the speaker; English is for all.

Unfortunately, there are many who criticize or even ridicule non-native speaker's English abilities. On the extreme side, some native English-speaking Americans are even intolerant of foreign accents or "broken English" holding on the xenophobic views in the form of "This is American! Speak American!". Others more commonly, while not explicitly showing bias towards non-native speakers, have subconscious tendencies to perceive foreign accents and speaking mannerisms in a negative way.

Whether explicit and implicit, these perceptions lead to linguistic discrimination and accent bias—a phenomena that marginalizes English language learners socially and limits their economic and educational opportunities in America. America has no place for such discrimination. Native English-speaking Americans need to acknowledge the universality of English, embrace the English and accents spoken by non-native speakers, and consciously move away from discriminatory perceptions and behaviors.

As Americans gain awareness of this issue, seek greater understanding of differing language and cultures, and advocate for progressive policies accepting English language learner's place in society, America can destigmatize foreign accents and speaking mannerisms, eliminating language discrimination and accent bias.

To put a face on the issue, let us look at one example in which we can see the effects of language bias and how to look past limited speaking ability. In her famous short work, " Mother Tongue", Amy Tan uses the example of her own mother to show the hardships and judgements faced by English language learners in American society and asserts her claim that English is individualistic with no one "proper" form. Throughout her life, Tan has observed her Mother's unique English and seen how others react to it. She recalls that, "people in department stores at banks, and at restaurants did not take her seriously, did not give her good services, pretended not to understand her, or even acted as if they did not hear her" on account of her imperfect English (Tan 2).

This social disservice to English language learners is widespread affecting people of all backgrounds. Tan also explains the negative perceptions of English language learners with her own thoughts growing up. She explains, "my mother's 'limited' English limited my perception of her . . . I believed that her English reflected the quality of what she had to say. That is, because she expressed them imperfectly her thoughts were imperfect" (Tan 2). While native speakers judged her mother's English, Tan realized her own familiarity with it. She has no trouble understanding the messages being conveyed by her Mother. In retrospect, her mother's English is quit natural to her and not "broken." She realized the richness behind her mother's "broken" English: "her intent, her passion, her imagery, the rhythms of her speech and nature of her thoughts" (Tan 3).

In making these points, Tan urges us to second language speakers as competent people with stories, opinions, and messages to be shared. Just as Tan has done before, we must empathize with English language learners, look past the cosmetics, and try to understand the speaker. Remember: there is a person behind the words we hear.

Instructor's Formative Assessment of Alexander's Half-Draft of Research Paper

Content

Note: 75% of grade.

- You wrote a half-draft meaningfully about need to address discrimination toward English Language Learners (ELL). Tone and vocabulary are pitched just right for your primary audience of Americans resistant to ELL usage of English, though there is much passive voice when a persuasive essay calls for directness or active voice.
- Good start with great hook, but several areas need your attention for revision:
    - Rephrase "Let's not . . . them": though true, different voice than rest of paper—bring it up a level.*
    - Thesis has a clear topic, but it's too ambitious for 6–8-page paper. To focus on three subtopics when each could be its own argument to fill the paper is concerning that all won't receive in-depth coverage. Quality over quantity.*
    - Qualify statements with some, mostly, mainly, at times, or other reference that steers away from absolutism—keep in mind for thesis as all Americans will not endeavor, unfortunately, and all language discrimination will not be eliminated, sadly.*

- Argument is quite repetitive about acceptance and discrimination. Spend more time on final draft deepening and varying your points as related to your thesis.
- Cite more studies of true problem in Lit. Review.* How damaging is the discrimination? Need to lean on sources to prove this (even though it seems obvious to the educated, reasonable person).*
- Can you find any sources that speak to the influx of ELL learners (refer to in your argument as this is current, accepted term)? Show the extent of ELL in America for, say, the last 2–3 decades. Then, build upon these stats to make your case.*
- Body paragraph is generally balanced with analysis and evidence; however, all body paragraphs need more extended analysis.
- Sources are limited. Only two truly credible; be wary of .com sites (yes, some are useful, but the purpose of the paper is to find scholarly sources/primary sources).*

Conventions

Note: 25% of grade.

- Cap: Xenophobic (proper noun)
- Reduce passive voice (reference lecture note from class)
- Intro. all quotes. (e.g., "Evaluations of language varieties . . .)
- Place commas inside quotes when no citations follow
- Punctuate titles of literature in work cited
- Use "ELLs" after you've introduced English Language Learners for the first time
- Verify MLA format in several of your works cited entries
- Watch overuse of these words: acceptance, it, but, this—use control 7 to locate and replace

*Indicates comments that Alexander addressed in his full draft. The only comment that Alexander did not address was adding more analysis to each body paragraph.

Alexander's Final Draft of Research Paper with Revisions Addressing Commentary

Who? Alexander, college freshman

What? Research paper on a social justice issue; 6–8 pages with at least six credible sources, including an interview with person who has expertise on the topic

When? Spring 2021

Where? Freshman English composition course at small New England College

Prompt: Take a position on a social justice issue in America and continue the persuasive argument that also includes a counterargument. Direct your argument toward a primary audience

*Bracketed words are sections that Alexander added in his final draft.

Lingua Franca: Speaking American

Improper grammar at times? Maybe. Unique pronunciation? Quite possibly. In your lifetime, you have likely had numerous interactions with people who speak English as a second language or with those trying their best to learn it. As anyone who has taken a beginner foreign language class much traveling to a foreign country where a different language is spoken know, speaking a non-native language is extremely difficult. Yes, improper grammar with its unique pronunciation tends to be characteristics of second language speakers' speech. It's is perfectly acceptable and understandable.

But how do these characteristics affect perceptions on non-native speakers? As research suggests, English language learners with foreign accents, often perceived unfairly as "broken English," are subject to negative bias leaning to linguistic discrimination. This stigma around their language ability marginalizes them socially and places disadvantages on career and educational advancement opportunities.

The language rooted in a wide spectrum of views ranging from xenophobic sentiments to subconscious bias, nonetheless, no matter where the bias lies on the spectrum, its discriminatory effects are unacceptable. [Some argue, English language learners should strive to master their language ability to succeed in America. Although there is some merit to the argument, people need acceptance; there is no reason for marginalization of English language learners.

Once American society recognizes those language biases and seeks to fully accept English language learners, they can begin to tackle these problems. In order to reduce language discrimination and accent bias in American, native English language speakers are responsible to recognize these issues and seek greater understanding of differing cultures and linguistics to ultimately embrace English language learners' place in American society.]

[To dive deeper into this discussion, we need to uncover the roots of this issue by examining where language biases come from. Although bigotry and xenophobia (fear of that which is foreign) contribute to some language discriminations, it does not account for much of the discrimination faced by second language speakers. Sarah Hansen, a language discrimination researcher, makes the point that "stereotyping issues" often arise from "an unconscious, socially constructed ideology based on deeply ingrained concepts of standardizing language that position linguistic discrimination as natural (Hansen 5).

This ideology, known as "Standard Language Ideology, "suggests that there is one correct form of English better than all others and when one evaluates speech in this manner, speakers of different varieties may also be evaluated based on their proximity or distance from the "standard" (Hansen 5).

Under "Standard Language Ideology," anyone with a differing accent, speaking mannerisms, or "broken English" is subject to subconscious judgments about their intelligence or character from the listener. This raises questions as to what "standard English" is and whether or not such a notion as "American English exists."]

As the most widely used language globally, English is often referred to as the universal business language. The demand for English speakers is, in fact, has created a large disparity between the number of native and non-native speakers. In an estimation, "roughly 70%" of more than a billion English speakers worldwide are not primary language speakers, but rather learned it as a second language (*Ethnologue*). Looking into American demographics, in 2018, there was a reported "44.8 million foreign immigrants living in the United States" (Budimann). [Within in the past few decades, United States immigration ttrends have seen a steep rise beginning in 1970 when immigrants made up "4.7%" of the U.S. population to 2019 where they contribute to "13.7%" of the total population (Migration).

These trends are anticipated to continue; by the year 2065, "among the projected 441 million Americans . . . 78 million will be immigrants and 81 million will be people born in the U.S. to immigrant parents" bringing the total immigrant population to "18%.' (Cohn 2).]

With these staggering statistics in mind, it only makes sense that there are numerous variations of the language distinct from what some would consider standard "American English". Differing accents and speaking mannerisms seems most natural coming from such a diverse population of English speakers, not to mention learners. [If English is, as these statitics show, the universal language, the minority population of primary English speakers must be flexible and accepting of the language characteristics of the diverse group of majority non-native speakers.]

While they rarely admit it as much, American Native English-speakers often take for granted that their native tongue is so widely spoken. English has become the default language to use when attempting to communicate with others. This fact, however, has led many Americans to become comfortable in the belief that "English is the standard" and has created unfair expectations for immigrants and foreigners in their English abilities.

The ease of communication through English has numbed monolinguistic native English speakers to the languages and backgrounds of others, while simultaneously developed impatience and resistance towards understanding less than perfect English. [When asked in an interview, "Do you think people have perceived or treated you differently based on your English?", a Mexican immigrant mother replied, "Yes. When we go to the bank or go the store, people don't speak to me very much because they think I won't understand. I think if I could speak better English, people might be more willing to talk, people would understand me" (Ramirez).] Rather than lending an ear in and seeking to understand others, many choose to keep walls of separation between their connections to others. Language barriers exist, but they can be deconstructed.

[While referencing a multitude of previous studies, Dr. Stephanie Lindemann, a sociolinguist, writes that "Research . . . in which listeners are asked to rate recorded speakers of different varieites on qualities such as intelligence and likeability, has shown that U.S. listeners actively evaluate (at least under some conditions) native speakers of Spanish and German, as well as Malaysians, Chinese, Japanese, Koreans, and Italians, Norwegians, and Eastern Europeans (Lindemann 12). The common threads in evaluations of language learners from varying geographical areas presents a strong link between perceptions of the speaker's language and perceptions of the speaker's native country. "Evaluations of language varieties can be understood as evaluations of the groups who speak them rather than the language *per se*" (Lindemann1).

In a study where undergraduates rated their foreign peers on their English based on categories of "correct, please friendly, and familiar", "groups that have been identified as non-stigmatized were rated positively (France, Germany), at least on correctness; groups that have been described as stigmatized (Mexico, Japan, China, India) were rated as 'less correct'" (Lindemann 6).

Innate factors surrounding the speaker's background, including national origin, can override the listener's impartial judgement of the speaker when the listener has preconceived notions antipathetic towards the speaker's background. Conclusively, listeners may dismiss the credibility of a non-native speaker or critically assess the speaker's language ability based on stereotypes of the speaker's ethnic background. These hasty generalizations hinder the listener from objectively listening and conversing with English language learners.]

In extreme cases, those who hold intolerant opinions such as "This is America, speak proper English!" or "Speak American!" end up building language barriers even higher. As it has been said repeatedly before, America is a melting pot. Ideally, diversity should be accepted. Language and culture identity should be accepted. Yet, xenophobic, and bigoted sentiments harm the melting pot.

All citizens, whether native-born or naturalized immigrants must be accepted. It would be counterintuitive for a diverse country like the United States, which does not have an official language, to reject or discriminate those who speak a mother tongue other than English. [Paragraph 2 from half-draft reduced and relocated to paragraph 5 in final draft]

To put a face on the issue, let us look at one example in which we can see the effects of language bias and how to look past limited speaking ability. In her famous short work, " Mother Tongue", Amy Tan uses the example of her own mother to show the hardships and judgements faced by English language learners in American society and asserts her claim that English is individualistic with no one "proper" form. Throughout her life, Tan has observed her Mother's unique English and seen how others react to it. She recalls that, "people in department stores at banks, and at restaurants did not take her seriously, did not give her good services, pretended not to understand her, or even acted as if they did not hear her" on account of her imperfect English (Tan 2).

This social disservice to English language learners is widespread affecting people of all backgrounds. Tan also explains the negative perceptions of English language learners with her own thoughts growing up. She explains, "my mother's 'limited' English limited my perception of her . . . I believed that her English reflected the quality of what she had to say. That is, because she expressed them imperfectly her thoughts were imperfect" (Tan 2).

While native speakers judged her mother's English, Tan realized her own familiarity with it. She has no trouble understanding the messages being conveyed by her Mother. In retrospect, her mother's English is quit natural to her and not "broken." She realized the richness behind her mother's "broken" English: ". . . her intent, her passion, her imagery, the rhythms of her speech and nature of her thoughts" (Tan 3). In making these points, Tan urges us to second language speakers as competent people with stories, opinions, and messages to be shared. Just as Tan has done before, we must empathize with English language learners, look past the cosmetics, and try to understand the speaker. Remember: there is a person behind the words we hear.

[Unknown to many Americans, the United States does not have an official language. Instead, it has a common language or lingua franca: English. The lingua franca allows ease of communication throughout the country. Just like any other language, English connects us to each other, helping to understand one another, voice opinions, tell stories, and conduct business.

Thus, residents in America should strive for the ability to speak English and speak well. To maintain English as the common language, consistency with the basic structure of the language required—its grammar, the definition of words, and basics phonetics of its alphabet.

Heterogeneity within language is required to meet the everyday linguistic needs of a community based on communication (Lippi-Green 25). Nonetheless, accents, differing speaking mannerisms, and even "broken English" should not be stigmatized or cause for linguistic discrimination. Language is fluid and individualistic to speaker.

Within English, there is ample room for language variation that will not damage the integrity of its structure or standing as the common language. Each speaker may use different words, sentences, sounds, intonations, imply different meanings with their language use, etc. because their language is unique to them (Lippi-Green 25).

Due to allowance for variation within the English language, such as a concept as a "singular standard English" that all conform to, cannot exist. Much less, there is no such thing as "speaking American." Understanding each other amongst differences is a two-way street where native speakers and secondary learners each have a part. As native speakers set out to be empathetic to learners and reduce biases, learners must work towards language adeptness to best integrate into an English filled America.]

[Unfortunately, many criticize or even ridicule non-native speaker's English abilities. On the extreme side, some native English-speaking Americans are even intolerant of foreign accents of "broken English" holding on to xenophobic views in the form of "This is America, speak American!" Others more commonly, while not explicitly showing bias toward non-native speakers, have subconscious tendencies to perceive foreign accents and speaking mannerisms in a negative way.

Whether explicit or implicit, these perceptions lead to linguistic discrimination and accent bias—a phenomena that marginalizes English language learners socially and limits their economic and educational opportunities in America. America has no place for such discrimination. Native English-speaking Americans need to acknowledge the multifaceted aspect of the English language, accept the diversity of speech patterns and accents spoken by non-native speakers, and consciously move away from discriminatory perceptions and behaviors.]

[As Americans gain awareness of this issue and seek greater understanding of differing language and cultures. America can destigmatize foreign accents and speaking mannerisms, reducing language discrimination and accent bias.]

Instructor's Summative Comments for Alexander's Final Draft of Research Paper

Topic and Rhetorical Approach

You've made a strong case for Americans to be mindful of their attitudes toward immigrants' and foreigners' use of English language that may be different from their own. Your primary audience of "monolinguistic Americans and those with little exposure to English language learner populations—a diverse population of Native-English speaking Americans throughout the country who may not realize the existence of linguistic discrimination and its associated biases" is clear and helps shape your argument convincingly.

You're right: compassion and understanding are key. As Amy Tan implied, their language is not "broken" but, rather, emerging as they learn nuances of speaking English. They deserve respect. Those of us who have traveled overseas know the humbling experience of coping with languages we have not yet mastered though need to function in interactions and everyday experiences. You serve as an advocate for the ELL community while also examining different viewpoints about the roots of linguistic discrimination and the most current ways to address this issue. Overall, clear purpose, less repetition, and major effort to revise since half-draft—and present a professional and mostly persuasive argument.

Content

Note: 75% of grade.

Stock comments with added words (noted in [brackets]) that tailor feedback to individual students. Bracketed items are comments that Alexander directly addressed from the instructor's feedback on the half-draft.

You've included a sharp introduction about ELLs with all necessary parts; amped up exigency [strongly]; swift transition to thesis; thesis is clear, arguable [(and indicative of many revisions; you've narrowed from an ambitious to a more streamlined one); you've also qualified statements to avoid absolutism]; Background/Lit. Review/Timeline [Time line now includes more about the influx of ELLs in the past few decades and used persuasively to build your side of the argument. However, in future papers, you'll need to collect 3–5 different sources to create a full literature review; yours is scattered]; body paragraphs have clear assertions (topic sentences) to support your thesis and adequate evidence.

Your primary audience would benefit from extended analysis in several body paragraphs (e.g., paragraph 4—deepen analysis about interview) and in rebuttal [last paragraph], specifically, elaborating on the logical fallacy and explaining how/why this exploits the counterargument. Paragraph 5, which is a syllogism, shows some understanding of ways this logic works in argument, but this is the [most feeble paragraph in argument—assertion/major premise comes "in back door"/be direct here, and minor premise needs to align more to major premise]

Furthermore, your interview added value to your argument with thoughtful questions that generated relevant content; conclusion is too brief and needs a serious call for action for ["Speaking American."]—don't miss this opportunity of a strong finish in fresh words. Source handling is mostly accurate, careful, and integrative. [Watch for leaning too hard on one source in given paragraphs; try to diversify. You've added more credible sources, thus increasing your own credibility.]

Quotes and paraphrases are acceptable and selected wisely in terms of source text to paraphrase and ways to boil down. [Most sentence-level issues (from half-draft)] addressed effort to use professional language, pay more attention to reducing passive voice (as we discussed in class); used appropriate vocabulary for the primary audience, and showed understanding that professional presentation requires great attention to detail. Though not without areas to sharpen, a very strong understanding of argument and rhetoric that will serve you well in future papers.

Conventions

Note: 25% of grade.

Comments for Half-Draft

- Cap: Xenophobic (proper noun)
- Reduce passive voice (reference lecture note from class)
- Introduce all quotes. (e.g., "Evaluations of language varieties . . .)
- Place commas inside quotes when no citations follow

168   APPENDIX B

- Punctuate titles of literature in works cited*
- Use "ELLs" after you've introduced English Language Learners for the first time
- Verify MLA format in several of your works cited entries
- Watch overuse of these words: acceptance, it, but, this—use control 7 to locate and replace* (to an extent).

*Only comments that Alexander addressed in the final draft

Comments for Final Draft

- Cap: Xenophobic (proper noun)
- Continue to reduce passive voice (reference lecture note from class)
- Introduce all quotes (e.g., "Evaluations of language varieties . . .)
- [Practice combining sentences (e.g., paragraph 8)]
- Place commas inside quotes when no citations follow
- Use "ELLs" after you've introduced English Language Learners for the first time
- Verify MLA format in several of your works cited entries

Alexander's Reflection on Instructor's Online Comments

When interviewed by author with this question, "Why did you do well on final draft" (earned a B+), Alexander said he understood his instructor's expectations within the comments, agreed with the majority of them, and understood that if he addressed the comments, his paper could be stronger. He also said he wanted to show good academic writing. As noted, Alexander did not address the majority of sentence-level issues.

In a post-paper interview, he responded to the question, "Why didn't you address more convention comments in your final draft?" with these words: "I don't have a trained eye yet to notice all these errors. I was so focused on the content, I forgot about them." This issue speaks to continuing struggles within the online environment in which students receive content and convention comments but tend to focus only on the content comments. To address this issue, a sentence-level exercise follows on the next page in which the instructor does not want the student to repeat the same kinds of errors in the next draft. Other approaches to sentence-level issues are discussed in chapter 5.

APPENDIX C

Case Study of Formative and Summative Online Comments for Rough and Final Drafts of Research Paper, Freshman History Course

Documents Present:

- Juan's rough draft with instructor's online comments
- Juan's final draft with instructor's online comments
- Analysis of impact of instructor's online comments
- Juan's reflection of online comments

Who? Juan, college freshman

What? Research paper on impactful American social movements; 3–4 pages

When? Spring 2021

Where? American social movements (history) course at small New England College

Prompt: Which American social movement had a strong, meaningful impact on the lives of its citizens? Why?

Juan's Rough Draft with Instructor's (Mrs. Barteaux) Online Comments

School Safety Movement

~~Growing up and going through the public-school system at the dawn of the 21st century, I can say from first-hand experience that nothing has had a more profound impact on my generation's educational experience than the constant threat and occurrences of school shootings. I feel as if everyone knows a person affected by these tragedies, and this has created a sense of fear among many young Americans. For example, I still remember where I was and what I was doing when I first heard of the Sandy Hook attack. The elementary school lied just thirty minutes west of my own. This dark day will forever be etched into my memory and in the memories of millions~~ **[MrsB1]**.

~~This~~ [The Sandy Hook] shooting along with dozens of others <u>has given</u> [PV instead, use "gave"] birth to the school safety movement, a movement made up of multiple groups ~~all~~ fighting to see the day where school shootings are no longer a lingering threat upon our nation's youth, teachers, school officials, and parents.

[MrsB1: Sorry, but this is research, not an essay. There are no pronouns I, me, we, she, it, they, them, theirs, etc.]

Many of [~~these~~] groups comprising the school safety movement <u>were founded</u> by students who sought change or <u>were personally impacted</u> by school shootings. The students who <u>have created</u> ~~these groups have been and~~ [advocate for school safety?] are ~~still~~ currently deprived of [their] right to ~~being~~ safe[ty] in public schools ~~and are tired of just waiting on the sidelines, so they decided to do something about it~~. This [The movement] <u>has become</u> the first movement in the United States with my generation at the helm and they are making ground against powerful adversaries. [Do you have evidence that this is the first movement run by young people? This sentence is editorializing and should be omitted.]

The school safety movement first appeared at the scene in 1997 after the Columbine school shooting and became fueled by the later Sandy Hook and Parkland shootings. Some of the early organizing groups include Sound and Safe Schools, School Safety Advocacy Council, Parkland School Safety Group and Never Again **[MrsB2]**. ~~Many of these groups are run by~~ [S]tudents ~~of~~ [from] schools [struck by] ~~where~~ tragedy has struck, such as the Never Again and Parkland School Safety Group [run]. . . . Even though these are different groups in their own right, the goals of the groups are closely aligned. **[MrsB3]**

Their [Whose?] goals are to create stricter background checks for gun buyers and limit what firearms may be bought to ~~achieve their overlying goal of~~ preventing future school shootings. The strategies used ~~by the different groups~~ are also similar and overlap. ~~By having similar goals and strategies, the different groups of the movement have founded~~ [Who formed] alliances ~~with each other~~.

Other allies of the movement are teachers and parents, who do not want to see their kids [children? Students?] in danger, and Democratic politicians who fight to strengthen gun laws. ~~The strategies used by the groups~~ [repetitive] include a strong social media presence, organized student walkouts, protests, and rallies. ~~These strategies~~ are intended [Who intends] to raise awareness for the government to pass legislation to make gun ownership harder, as well as raise public awareness ~~of the general public~~ that students want ~~to see a change so they can have their~~ the right to safe schooling. The most successful walkout conducted by the movement was named ENOUGH. It was created ~~by~~ Organizers of the Women March Youth EMPOWER group~~, and they~~ called for students, teachers, school administrators, parents, and allies to take part in a [#NationalSchoolWalkout].

[MrsB2: Is there a link between Columbine activism and the movement twenty years later? You are lumping "many groups" together. Who was first? Columbine? Sandy Hook? Develop that group's activism. Then, move on to newer groups (allies), and as you raise a group explain the strategies the group used.]

[MrsB3: Almost all the language used so far has been riddled with vague pronouns, passive voice, and unnecessary language that does not provide the reader with direct information. This paper will need intensive revision to simplify language and reorganize for clarity.]

~~For 17 minutes at 10 a.m.~~ On March 14, 2018, across every time zone [Empower requested participants to walkout for 17 minutes at 10 a.m. CITE] The 17 minutes represented the 17 people who had lost their lives at the Parkland shooting (Regis University). [It was part of the memory of a memorial? To victims] ~~those who had passed away,~~ but ~~it was~~ also a protest for ~~a~~ change ~~that the country desired~~ [MrsB4]-[MrsB5]

The school safety movement ~~has been met~~ with many forms of resistance. The biggest threats to the movement's agenda consist of the ~~second amendment,~~ [MrsB6] the NRA, the Republican party and some school districts.

The United States Constitution explicitly states, in the second amendment of the Bill of Rights[, that citizens have] "A right to bear arms.". Many Americans take this amendment ~~very~~ seriously and ~~truly~~ believe that ~~any~~ American[s have] ~~has~~ the right to possess ~~any~~ weapons. Hours after surviving the Parkland shooting, Cameron Kasky, the student co-founder of the Never Again group stated ~~on Facebook~~, "Thank you to all of the second amendment warriors who protected me" (The New Yorker).

~~This was obvious~~ [Kasky's] sarcasm ~~on the part of the student because~~ [referred to the fact that] no one was there to protect ~~him,~~[students,] rather the second amendment ~~just~~ made it easier for the school shooter, Nikolas Cruz, to obtain the AR-15 he ~~eventually~~ used to shoot up the school. ~~This was a~~ [Students'] shared frustration ~~among the students,~~ as Alfonso Calderon, another cofounder of Never Again ~~group told The New Yorker that~~ [claimed], "We have to vote people out who have been paid for by the NRA. They're allowing this to happen. They are making it easier for people like Nick Cruz to obtain an AR-15"(The New Yorker). The

[MrsB4: School shooting movement meets social movement criteria.]

[MrsB5: There is no sense of who is doing what. Need to develop early organization and the activism of individual and group allies. –6]

[MrsB6: The Second Amendment cannot be an active opponent, instead it is an argument used by opponents.]

students within the School Safety movement see the NRA as responsible for funding ~~many~~ pro-gun candidates ~~to run~~ for office to keep gun control limited. Most of these government officials are Republicans and preserving the second amendment is a cornerstone of the Republican party. [Cite] The Republican party <u>has controlled</u> at least one of the houses of [Congress (since when?)] ~~and this has made passing legislation to create gun control very difficult for the movement and their allies~~ [making it difficult to pass gun control legislation.

Certain school?] districts around the country ~~have~~ also aligned ~~themselves~~ against the movement. ~~The University of San Francisco Law review stated,~~ [MrsB7] "Other schools reacted differently by outright disallowing their students from any sort of involvement with the walkouts" (Solange Tadros). [Where was this and when?] Besides being an infringement on the students's first amendment [rights], ~~as stated by the review,~~ the school systems <u>were attempting</u> to suppress the message of the school safety movement. [cite]

[MrsB7: No need to cite sources in the research, that is what citations are for.]

Despite the drawback of their opposition, the movement <u>has made</u> progress in politically enacting gun control laws across the country. After the Parkland shooting, "Florida Gov. Rick Scott on Friday signed a measure that, among other things, raises the minimum age to purchase a gun from 18 to 21" (Los Angeles Times). [This] <u>was followed</u> by multiple other states creating stricter gun laws such as Colorado (CNN). Republican President Trump <u>has even complied</u> to increase gun laws through the creation of 'red flag' gun laws (CNN). [What is a red flag law?][MrsB8]Despite being predominantly run by students and having to go against ~~some~~ [one?] of the largest interest groups in the U.S., the school safety movement <u>has been</u> successful in pushing the states and federal governments to create [a few?]

[MrsB8: Explain red flag law or omit.]

stricter gun laws so that schools around the country are safer **[MrsB9]**.

Citations

Dezenski, Lauren. "Trump Backs 'Red Flag' Gun Laws. What Do They Actually Do?" *CNN*, Cable News Network, 6 Aug. 2019, www.cnn.com/2019/08/05/politics/red-flag-gun-law-explainer-donald-trump/index.html.

"The NRA Says Florida's Law Raising the Age Limit on Buying Guns Is Unconstitutional. But Is It?" *Los Angeles Times*, Los Angeles Times, 13 Mar. 2018, www.latimes.com/nation/la-na-florida-gun-law-20180312-htmlstory.html.

Redirecting . . ., heinonline.org/ HOL/Page?collection=journals&handle=hein.journals%2Fusflr53&id=507&men_tab=srchresults. **[MrsB10]**

Witt, Emily, et al. "How the Survivors of Parkland Began the Never Again Movement." *The New Yorker*, www.newyorker.com/news/news-desk/how-the-survivors-of-parkland-began-the-never-again-movement.

[MrsB9: There is good coverage of exclusion, goals, strategies, and collision. Good use of quotes. There are missing citations. –1 Passive voice is underlined and must be revised to active. Omit highlighted pronouns that are vague and require unnecessary language. Omit repetitive phrases. Please read all comments and notes in paper. You need to significant editing to bring clarity to research. –8 Paper is over word count. –2]

[MrsB10: This is an inaccurate citation. Fix. You are missing a scholarly journal as the information and link provided are not accurate.]

Juan's Final Draft with Instructor's (Mrs. Barteaux) Online Comments

School Safety Movement

The Parkland shooting along with dozens of other [MrsB11] gave birth to the school safety movement, a movement made up of multiple groups fighting to see the day where school shootings are no longer a lingering threat upon our nation's youth, teachers, school officials, and parents. Many of the groups comprising the school safety movement *was founded PV* by students who sought change or have been personally impacted by school shootings. The students who advocate for school safety are currently deprived of a right to safety in public schools.

Some of the early organizing groups of the school safety movement include Sound and Safe Schools, School Safety Advocacy Council, [MrsB12] Parkland School Safety Group and Never Again. These groups got involved in the movement after the Parkland shooting and set the foundation for the modern school safety movement. Students from Parkland formed many of the underlying groups such as Never Again and Parkland School Safety Group. Even though these are different groups in their own right, the goals of the groups are similar and hence they are aligned together to form the backbone of the school safety movement. The school safety movement's goals are to create stricter background checks for gun buyers and limit what firearms may be bought to prevent future school shootings. [MrsB13] Alongside students, the movement is aligned with teachers and parents, who do not want to see children in danger, and Democratic politicians who fight to strengthen gun laws.

[MrsB11: This is an inaccurate citation. Fix. You are missing a scholarly journal as the information and link provided are not accurate. Missing word: shootings.]

[MrsB12: Why do you include these groups if you never discuss them? Did they come before Parkland groups? Did Parkland align with them to learn from them? Unclear whether these organizations are allies or what their roles are in activism.]

[MrsB13: Only goal is gun related.]

The school safety movement uses a strong social media presence and the power to organize student walkouts, protests and rallies as its main strategy to accomplish its goal of strengthening gun laws. The school safety movement intends to use these strategies to raise awareness **[MrsB14]** for the government to pass legislation to make gun ownership harder, as well as raise public awareness that students have the right to safe schooling.

[MrsB14: Another goal?]

The most successful walkout conducted by the movement is named ENOUGH. ENOUGH is the creation of the Organizers of the Women March Youth EMPOWER group which called for students, teachers, school administrators, parents, and allies to take part in a #NationalSchoolWalkout. On March 14, 2018, across every time zone. EMPOWER requested participants to walkout for 17 minutes at 10 a.m (Regis University). The 17 minutes represented theeoplee who had lost their lives at the Parkland shooting (Regis University). The walk out was a memorial to the victims; but also a protest for a change.

The school safety movement is sieged **[MrsB15]** by many forms of resistance. The biggest threats to the movement's agenda consist of the NRA, the Republican party and some school districts. The United States Constitution explicitly states, in the second amendment of the Bill of Rights that citizens have "A right to bear arms." Many Americans take this amendment seriously and believe that Americans have the right to possess weapons. Hours after surviving the Parkland shooting, Cameron Kasky, the student co-founder of the Never Again group stated, "Thank you to all of the second amendment warriors who protected me" (The New Yorker). Kasky's sarcasm referred to the fact that no one was there to protect students, rather the second amendment made it easier for the school shooter, Nikolas Cruz, to obtain the AR-15 he used to shoot up the school.

[MrsB15: Do you mean besieged? Maybe not the best word for this.]

Students' shared frustration, as Alfonso Calderon, another cofounder of Never Again claimed, "We have to vote people out who have been paid for by the NRA. They're allowing this to happen. They are making it easier for people like Nick Cruz to obtain an AR-15" (The New Yorker). The students within the School Safety movement see the NRA as responsible for funding pro-gun candidates for office to keep gun control limited. Most of these government officials are Republicans and preserving the second amendment is a cornerstone of the Republican party (CNN). The Republican party *have controlled PV* at least one of the houses of Congress since making **[MrsB16]** it difficult to pass gun control legislation.

[MrsB16: Since what?]

Certain school districts around the country also aligned against the movement. "Other schools reacted differently by outright disallowing their students from any sort of involvement with the walkouts" (Solange Tadros). An example of this occurred in the Des Moines Independent School District during the ENOUGH walkout in 2018(Solange Tadros). Besides being an infringement on the student's first amendment rights the school systems attempted to suppress the message of the school safety movement.

Despite the drawback of their **[MrsB17]** opposition, the movement is making progress in politically enacting gun control laws across the country.After the Parkland shooting, "Florida Gov. Rick Scott on Friday signed a measure that, among other things, raises the minimum age to purchase a gun from 18 to 21" (Los Angeles Times). Florida's law change led to multiple other states creating stricter gun laws such as Colorado (CNN). Even Republican President Trump agreed to increase gun laws through the creation of 'red flag' gun laws (CNN). Red flag laws are described as, "State laws that authorize courts to issue a special type of

[MrsB17: Wrong word.]

protection order, allowing the police to temporarily confiscate firearms from people who are deemed by a judge to be a danger to themselves or to others" (New York Times). [MrsB18]Despite being predominantly run by students and having to go against one of the largest interest groups in the U.S., the school safety movement was successful in pushing the states and federal governments to create a few stricter gun laws so that schools around the country are safer [MrsB19].

[MrsB18: Good!]

[MrsB19: Paper still has some unnecessary language, passive voice, and paragraphing issues.]

Citations

Braun, Eric. *Never Again: The Parkland Shooting and the Teen Activists Leading a Movement*. Lerner Publications, 2019.

Dezenski, Lauren. "Trump Backs 'Red Flag' Gun Laws. What Do They Actually Do?" *CNN*, Cable News Network, 6 Aug. 2019, www.cnn.com/2019/08/05/politics/red-flag-gun-law-explainer-donald-trump/index.html.

Tadros, Solange. "# Enough: A Look at Students' Seventeen Minute Walkouts following the Parkland Shooting and the First Amendment." *USFL Rev.* 53 (2019): 489.

"The NRA Says Florida's Law Raising the Age Limit on Buying Guns Is Unconstitutional. But Is It?" *Los Angeles Times*, Los Angeles Times, 13 Mar. 2018, www.latimes.com/nation/la-na-florida-gun-law-20180312-htmlstory.html.

Williams, Timothy. "What Are 'Red Flag' Gun Laws, and How Do They Work?" *The New York Times*, The New York Times, 6 Aug. 2019, www.nytimes.com/2019/08/06/us/red-flag-laws.html.

Witt, Emily, et al. "How the Survivors of Parkland Began the Never Again Movement." *The New Yorker*, www.newyorker.com/news/news-desk/how-the-survivors-of-parkland-began-the-never-again-movement.

GRADING RUBRIC FROM MRS. BARTEAUX

American Social Movement Process with Evidence and Analysis (70 points)	American Social Movement (History) Paper Process and Argument (40 points) • The introduction states why the movement meets the course definition of a "social movement." *See the syllabus for a complete definition.* • The thesis, introduction, body, and conclusion address and incorporate the GUF—directly or via stages of your narrative (creation of exclusion/oppression, realization of exclusion, early local organizing/mobilizing, etc.) • Your argument is cogent; through the complete GUF process and use of appropriate sources, you successfully demonstrate who, how, and why this Othered group, excluded from full participation in the pursuit of freedom and full citizenship, actively defined itself, organized to pursue its rights, and openly challenged the "In" system to achieve its goals. Research and Evaluation of Sources (30 points) • You use at least three outside sources: You must use at least one published scholarly monograph by a valid press or one journal article from a scholarly journal. You must include *at least one* primary source in your paper, outside of the readings in the course. Once you have the required monograph/journal and primary source, you may use other reliable sources, including internet sites. Check the assignment for more information on reliable sources. The paper should properly introduce appropriate evidence from your sources to enhance your argument (e.g., your evidence/source should support the point you are trying to make via direct quote or paraphrase).
Organization and Syntax (15 points)	• The paper meets the formatting requirements and conforms to the style sheet in D2L. • The paper is within the word count range (600–800 draft), (800–1,000 final). • The paper uses correct grammar and spelling, clear language, and careful word choice. The paper follows a logical structure, using paragraphs and topic sentences, while avoiding contractions, passive voice, and the use of impact as a verb. • The paper has been carefully proofread.
Documentation (10 points)**	• The paper cites sources according to MLA style and includes a proper works cited page. • The paper uses only sources from course materials and acceptable sources.
Revisions (5 points)	• Each draft incorporates feedback from the peer review session (mandatory) and peer tutors, HWRC, and instructor (as applicable).

**Papers significantly deficient in proper documentation will receive no higher than a 50.

Analysis of the Impact of Mrs. Barteaux's Online Comments

In the rough draft, the instructor had crossed out 33 groups of words that Juan did not add back in his final draft. Of 11 major comments on content, Juan addressed 9 in his final draft. He did not address the comments about citation of scholarly research and clarity about organizational allies. Of 19 comments on conventions, they were mainly focused on passive voice, use of demonstrative pronouns, and pronoun "their" in the topic sentence of paragraph 5. There were 13 instances of passive voice and 5 demonstrative pronouns in the rough draft whereas there were only 2 instances of passive voice and 2 demonstrative pronouns in the final draft. Overall, he addressed 74% of convention comments.

The content comments that Juan addressed in the final draft include rewrote introductory paragraph, narrowed focus, eliminated unnecessary information, addressed more key issues, and added both a definition and a scholarly source. The conventions comments that Juan addressed were mainly less passive voice and demonstrative pronouns as well as other minor edits at the sentence level. Juan addressed many of his instructor's comments, that is, he made many revisions, and his draft became substantially stronger in its focus, depth, and clarity.

Juan's Reflection on Mrs. Barteaux's Formative and Summative Commentary

During an interview, the author asked Juan why he did well on the final draft (earned an A–), and he said he followed Mrs. Barteaux's advice because she was thorough and took time to "care" about his paper, and he understood (generally) her expectations. Further, he agreed with the majority of comments and understood that they would make his paper stronger. However, he felt somewhat upset when he saw many lines crossed out, thinking, *I really messed up, especially the first eight lines*, then he told himself, "I have work to do, and, at least Mrs. Barteaux made these edits, and I'll build from there." He appreciated the one compliment of "good," saying "this gives me motivation, and it's good to know when you get something right." When asked why he did not address sentence-level comments, he said he "focused mainly on the bigger issues." Overall, Juan took Mrs. Barteaux's advice, and this paid dividends on his final draft, which was more streamlined, organized, and detailed than his rough draft.

APPENDIX D

Student Survey
Writing Practices and the Feedback Process

1. What are your beliefs about "good writing?"

For questions 2 through 12, choose past writing-based course(s) to reflect upon.

2. Think about the last time you received feedback on a paper. Why did you accept and/or reject major points of feedback?
3. Which approaches to feedback have you found beneficial? Or, comments I found useful . . .
4. Which approaches to feedback have you found frustrating? Or, comments I found least useful . . .
5. Have you received feedback in digital formats: audiotaped, videotaped, online postings, and/or other mode?
6. What are types of feedback have you received on content at the paper or essay level (overall)? Examples include organization/structure, audience awareness, purpose, hook, introduction, thesis statement, topic sentences, evidence, incorporating research, analysis, facts, depth of research, voice, and other elements.
7. Which type of feedback have you received on content at the paragraph level?
8. Which type of feedback have you received on citation styles such as MLA, APA, Chicago, or other?
9. What type of feedback have you received on conventions (grammar and punctuation)?

10. Describe any ways you have addressed feedback at the paper and/or paragraph level.
11. Describe any ways you have addressed feedback at the sentence level.
12. Have you used your instructor's comments in subsequent drafts? If "yes," how? If "no," why not?

Bibliography

Adcroft, Andy. (2011). "The Mythology of Feedback." *Higher Education Research and Development* 30(4): 405–419.
Bitzer, Lloyd. (1968). "The Rhetorical Situation." *Philosophy and Rhetoric* 1(1): 1–14.
Black, P., and D. William. (1998). "Assessment and Classroom Learning." *Assessment in Education* 5(1): 7–74.
Boud, D. (1995). "Assessment and Learning: Contradictory or Complementary?" In P. Knight (Ed.), *Assessment and Learning in Higher Education*, 38–48. London: Kogan Page.
Brackett, Marc. "Feelings Influence Decisions." Marcbrackett.com, 10 November 2019. https://www.marcbrackett.com/feelings-influence-decisions/. Accessed 30 December 2020.
Brackett, Marc. (2020). *Permission to Feel*. New York: Celadon.
Brackett, Marc. (2019). *Permission to Feel: Unlocking the Power of Emotions to Help Our Kids, Ourselves, and Our Society Thrive*. New York: Celadon.
Brookhart, Susan M. (2016). *Giving Students Effective Feedback*. Alexandria, VA: Association for Supervision and Curriculum Development.
Brookhart, Susan M. (2013). *How to Create and Use Rubrics for Formative Assessment and Grading*. Alexandria, VA: Association for Supervision and Curriculum Development.
Brucker, Jacob. Interview, 15 November 2019.
Carless, David. (2006). "Differing Perceptions in the Feedback Process." *Studies in Higher Education* 31(2): 219–233.
Connors, Robert J., and Andrea Lunsford. (1988). "Frequency of Formal Errors in Current College Writing, or Ma and Pa Kettle Do Research." *College Composition and Communication* 39(4): 395–409.

Corbett, Edward P. J., and Robert J. Connors. (1998). *Classic Rhetoric for the Modern Student*, 4th ed. Oxford, UK: Oxford University Press.

Crimmins, G., G. Nash, F. Oprescu, M. Liebergreen, J. Turley, R. Bond, and J. Dayton. (2016). "A Written, Reflective, and Dialogic Strategy for Assessment Feedback That Can Enhance Student/Teacher Relationships." *Assessment and Evaluation in Higher Education* 41(1): 141–153.

Dowden, Tony, Sharon Pittawy, Helen Yost, and Robyn McCarthy. (2013). "Students' Perceptions of Written Feedback in Teacher Education: Ideally Feedback Is a Continuing Two-Way Communication That Encourages Progress." *Assessment and Evaluation in Higher Education* 38(1): 349–362.

Elbow, Peter. (1983). "Embracing Contraries in the Teaching Process." *College English* 45(4): 327–339.

Ferrell, G. (2013). "Supporting Assessment and Feedback Practice with Technology: From Tinkering to Transformation." Jisc Assessment and Feedback Programme. http://repository.jisc.ac.uk/5450/. Accessed 15 October 2019.

"Giving Students Feedback on Their Writing." Gale Morris Sweetland Center for Writing. University of Michigan, 2021. https://lsa.umich.edu/sweetland/instructors/teaching-resources/giving-feedback-on-student-writing.html. Accessed 18 February 2021.

Gray, Lisa. (2015). "Feedback and Feed Forward." JISC, 9 October 2015. Updated 20 April 2016. https://www.jisc.ac.uk/guides/transforming-assessment-and-feedback/feedback. Accessed 14 February 2021.

Hattie, John, and Shirley Clarke. (2019). *Visible Learning Feedback*. New York: Routledge.

Harvard Business Review. (2016). *HBR Guide to Delivering Effective Feedback: Boost Employee Performance, Communicate Openly, and Reinforce Established Goals*. Boston: Harvard Review Press.

Higgins, R., P. Hartley, and A. Skelton. (2002). "The Conscientious Consumer: Reconsidering the Role of Assessment Feedback in Student Learning." *Studies in Higher Education* 27(1): 53–64.

Higgins, R., P. Hartley, and A. Skelton (2001). "Getting the Message Across: The Problem of Communicating Assessment Feedback." *Teaching in Higher Education* 6(2): 269–274.

James, R., K.-L. Krause, and C. Jennings (2010). *The First-Year Experiences in Australian Universities: Findings from 1994–2009*. Melbourne: Centre for Higher Education Studies, University of Melbourne.

Kübler-Ross, Elisabeth, and David Kessler. (2014). *On Grief and Grieving: Finding the Meaning of Grief Through the Five Stages of Loss*. New York: Charles Scribner's Sons.

Lucas, George. (2021). "Why Is Assessment Important?" George Lucas Educational Foundation, Edutopia. https://www.edutopia.org/assessment-guide-importance. Accessed 18 February 2021.

Lunsford, Ronald F. (1997). "When Less Is More: Principles for Responding in the Disciplines." *New Directions for Teaching and Learning* 69: 91–104.

Maimon, Elaine, Janice Peritz, and Kathleen Blake-Yancey. (2009). *A Writer's Resource: A Handbook for Writing and Research*. New York: McGraw-Hill.

Mayer, J. D., and Salovey, P. (1997). "What Is Emotional Intelligence?" In P. Salovey and D. J. Sluyter (Eds.), *Emotional Development and Emotional Intelligence: Educational Implications*. New York: Basic Books.

McGee, Patty. (2017). *Feedback That Moves Writers Forward: How to Escape Correcting Mode to Transform Student Writing*. Newbury Park, CA: Corwin.

Merry, S., P. Orsmond, and D. Galbraith. (2007). "Does Providing Academic Feedback to Students Via Mp3 Audio Files Enhance Learning?" HEA Centre for Bioscience. http://www.bioscience.heacademy.ac.uk/resources/projects/merry.aspx. Accessed 15 October 2019.

Nicol, D. J. (2010). "From Monologue to Dialogue: Improving Written Feedback Processes in Mass Higher Education." *Assessment and Evaluation in Higher Education* 35(5): 501–517.

Nicol, D. J., and D. Macfarlane-Dick. (2006). "Formative Assessment and Self-Regulated Learning: A Model and Seven Principles of Good Feedback Practice." *Studies in Higher Education* 31(2): 199–218.

Penaflorida. "The Role of Teacher in Written Feedback." UKessays.com, 11 April 2018. https://www.ukessays.com/essays/education/the-role-of-teacher-written-feedback-education-essay.php?vref=1. Accessed 18 February 2021.

Pintrich, P. R., and A. Zusho. (2002). "Student Motivation and Self-Regulated Learning in the College Classroom." In J. C. Smart and W. G. Tierney (Eds.), *Higher Education: Handbook of Theory and Research* (vol. XVII). New York: Agathon Press.

Pollari, Pirjo. (2017). "To Feed Back or to Feed Forward? Students' Experiences of Responses to Feedback in the Finnish EFL Classroom: Engineering." *Apples: Journal of Applied Language Skills* 11(4): 11–33. https://doi.org/10.17011/apples/urn.201708073429. Accessed 27 June 2020.

Price, Margaret, Karen Handley, Jill Millar, and Berry O'Donovan. (2010). "Feedback: All That Effort, But What Is the Effect?" *Assessment and Evaluation in Higher Education* 35(3): 277–289.

Rodway-Dyer, Sue, Jasper Knight, and Elizabeth Dunne. (2011). "A Case Study on Audio Feedback with Geography Undergraduates." *Journal of Geography in Higher Education* 35(2): 217–231.

Sheldon, Oliver, Daniel Ames, and David Dunning. (2014). "Unskilled, Unaware, and Uninterested in Learning More: Reactions to Emotional Intelligence Feedback." *Journal of Applied Psychology* 99(1): 125–137. https://doi.org/10.1037/a0034138. Accessed 27 June 2020.

Sommers, Nancy. (2013). *Responding to Student Writers.* New York: Bedford/St. Martin's.

Stevens, Dannelle D., and Antonia J. Levi. (2013). *Introduction to Rubrics: An Assessment Tool to Save Grading Time, Convey Effective Feedback, and Promote Student Learning*, 2nd ed. Sterling, VA: Stylus.

Straub, Richard, and Ronald F. Lunsford. (1995). *12 Readers Reading: Responding to College Student Writing.* Medford, NJ: Hampton.

Värlander, Sara. (2008). "The Role of Students' Emotions in Formal Feedback Situations." *Teaching in Higher Education* 13(2): 145–156.

Wink, Karen A. (1999). "Examining Perceptions: A Teacher and Students Negotiate Meaning of the Rhetorical Situation During the Response Process in an Advanced Composition Class." University of Maryland, PhD dissertation.

Index

Note: Page numbers in *italics* refer to figures.

abbreviations, 158, 159, 166, 168
abstract audiences, xi
academic language, 80
academic voices, 7
academic writing process, 7
affective domain, 116. *See also* emotional component
affective qualities, 151
alignment, 10; of written commentary, 74
analysis, xi, 38, 112–13; in commenting vocabulary description, 58, 63–64; in questions, 60; short story, *78–79*, *97*, 99
analytic rubrics, 41
applicability, xiii
archetypes, 81–82
assess, understand, and plan approach (AUP), 130, *130–31*, 131
assessments: commentary related to, 28; definition of, 26, 151; development from, 34; evaluation compared to, 26; informal and formal, 27; process in, 26; as proof, 25; purpose of, 25, 34; questions related to, 25. *See also* formative assessment; summative assessments
audiences, xi; in case study, English composition final draft, 165, 167; concept of, 15; for high-school and first-year college, 15; letter writing to, 16; for nonfiction persuasive paper, *99*, 100; pedagogical approach to, 16; primary, 5, 16, 17, *39*, 51, 57, 59, 61–62, 65; rhetoric on, 17; in rough and final drafts, 85, *85*; rubrics for, 16; secondary, 6–7, 17; social media as, 16
audio commentary, 89–113; advantages of, 89; benefits of, 91; classroom dialogue in, 98; classroom discussions related to, 89; confusion from, 99, *99*; as conversations, 93; dialogue in, 89; encouragement in, 95; factors related to, 90; first negative views

187

of, 94; first positive views of, 92–93; on freshman gender studies course, 101–8; grammar mistakes in, 99, *99*; in-depth detail of, 91; individualization of, 92; negative views of, 92; on nonfiction persuasive paper, 99, *99*, 100; numbered paragraphs in, 93, 95; objective related to, 90; online technology for, 95; participation in, 89, 91; positive views of, 91–92; preference for, 94, 113; questions and, 92; reasons for, 89; "recap" in, 95; repetitions of, 93, 94; responsibility in, 91; sample template for, 95–96; on short story analysis, *97*, 99; taxonomies in, 96–99, *97*, 100–101; template for, 101; time for, 100–101; tips for, 95; tone and expression in, *97*, 98; tone in, 90–91; understanding of, 92, 93; writing of, 92, 93, 94
audio commentary, case study #1, 101–8; audio comments transcript on, 103–5; content in, 101, 107; conventions in, 107; documents in, 101; ending in, 104; expansion in, 104; expectations in, 102–3, 105; final draft in, 105–7; final paragraph in, 104; in-person comments compared to, 108; logic in, 106; numbered paragraphs in, 101, 103; personal experience in, 102–3, 104, 105–6; polarities in, 103, 106; prompt in, 102; punctuation in, 106, 107; quotes in, 102, 103, 104; rough draft of, 102–3; sentence-level issues in, 104–5; student reflection on, 107–8; summary on, 105; thesis in, 104, 107; vocabulary in, 105, 107; who, what, when, where related to, 101; written commentary compared to, 107
audio commentary, case study #2: audio comments transcript in, 110–11; consistency in, 111; content in, 110, 112–13; conventions in, 111, 113; documents in, 108; final draft in, 111–12; impact analysis of, 112–13; philosophy in, 110, 112–13; prompt in, 108, 110; repetition in, 110, 112–13; rough draft in, 108–9; student reflection on, 113; thesis in, 110, 112–13; voices in, 111, 113; who, what, when, where related to, 108
audio comments transcripts, 103–5, 110–11
AUP. *See* assess, understand, and plan approach

Barteaux, Mrs. *See* case study, research paper
biases, 11, 120–21, 155–58
bidirectionality, 151
blind copies, 11
blog posts summative comments: academic language in, 80; clarification in, 82; conclusion in, 83; contextualization in, 82; contradictions in, 82; focus in, 83; hero concept in, 82–83; inconsistency in, 83; more credible sources in, 80; pivoting in, 82; sample draft related to, 81–82; sentence-level issues

in, 81; topic sentences in, 80;
  unifying element in, 83
Brackett, Marc, 120

capitalization, 76
Carless, David, 115
case study, English composition
  final draft: abbreviations in, 168;
  antithesis in, 160–61; audience
  in, 165, 167; conclusion in,
  165, 167; content of, 166–67;
  conventions of, 167; diversity
  in, 164–65; empathy in, 164;
  evidence in, 161–63; examples
  in, 162–64; expansion in, 161,
  167; generalizations in, 163;
  heterogeneity in, 164–65;
  intolerance in, 165; introduction
  in, 160; literature review in, 166–
  67; perceptions in, 163; personal
  experience in, 163–64; quotes and
  paraphrases in, 167, 168; research
  in, 162–63; sentence fragment in,
  165; standards in, 161; statistics
  in, 161–62; summation in,
  164–65; summative comments
  on, 166–67; theme in, 161; thesis
  in, 160, 166; topic and rhetorical
  approach of, 166; who, what,
  when, where, prompt in, 160
case study, English composition
  half-draft: abbreviations in, 168;
  accountability in, 154; biases in,
  155–58; "broken English" in,
  155, 156–58; conventions in, 159;
  documents in, 154; efficiency
  in, 153; English as standard in,
  156; final draft in, 153; formative
  assessment of, 158–59; grades
  in, 153; half-draft in, 153–58;
  punctuation in, 167–68; repetition
  in, 159; social disservice in, 157–
  58; "stock" comments in, 153;
  term overuse in, 168; topics in,
  158; universal business language
  in, 155; voices in, 159; who,
  what, when, where, prompt in,
  154; worldwide English speakers
  in, 155–56
case study, research paper:
  documents for, 169; grading
  rubric, 179; who, what, when,
  where, prompt for, 169
case study, research paper final draft
  online comments: appreciation of,
  180; impact of, 180; incoherence
  in, *176*; lack of clarity in, *175*,
  177; praise in, *178*, 180; PV in,
  175, 177, *178*; student reflection
  on, 180; understanding of, 180;
  word choice in, *176*, *177*; word
  omission in, 175, *175*
case study, research paper rough
  draft, 170–74; citations in, 173,
  173, 174, *174*; connections in,
  172, *172*; editorialization in, 170;
  essay compared to, *170*; evidence
  in, *170*; inaccuracy in, *174*; link
  in, *171*; logic in, 172, *172*; praise
  in, *174*; PV in, 170, 171, *171*,
  174; red flag law in, 173, *173*;
  repetition in, 171, *174*; social
  movement criteria in, *172*
case study final draft reflection:
  convention comments in, 168;
  sentence-level issues in, 167, 168
circle errors, 65–66
citations, 173, *173*, 174, *174*
clarity, 54–55, 62, 63, *175*, *177*
Clarke, Shirley, 1

Classic Rhetoric for the Modern Student (Corbet and Connors), 5–6, *6*
code switching, 7
cognitive skills, 141, 151
coherent thesis statements, 36
comic strip, *8*
commas, 69, 72, 145
comma splice (CS), 70
commentary, 28
commenting vocabulary, xiii, 49–72; authoritative and interactive balance in, 53; balance in, 53, *54*; clarity of, 54–55; conversational and formal balance, 53; copy editing in, 50; definition of, 57; DID acronym in, 54; editing logs in, 67; effectiveness of, 53; emotional response to, 52; framework for, 49; grades related to, 51, 52; instructor role in, 50–51; list common errors in, 66; main objective of, 50; main tenet of, 49; motivation in, 50–51; patterns and three-step approach in, 65–66; peer editing in, 67; primary audience in, 51; priorities in, 51, 52; punctuation in, 68; return papers without grades in, 67; sentence-level exercise in, 67–68; sentence-level issues in, 50, 52; specificity in, 55–56; spelling in, 55–56; student expectations and, 51; students' ally in, 49; 20 most common student errors in, 68–72; types of comments in, 53, *54*; on unnecessary words, 56; vague compared to specific comments in, 55–56; on verb specificity, 56
commenting vocabulary description, 57–64; analysis constructive feedback in, 63–64; analysis in, 58, 63–64; analysis questions in, 60; assignment in, 61, 62; clarity in, 62, 63; conciseness in, 63; constructive feedback in, 60–64; conventions comments in, 64–65; definition in, 57; distractions in, 61; evidence constructive feedback in, 63; evidence in, 58, 63; evidence questions in, 59–60; examples in, 63; expectations in, 61; grammar in, 64–65; logic in, 63; message or thesis constructive feedback in, 62; message or thesis in, 58; message or thesis questions in, 59; opposing argument in, 64; opposing audience in, 62; optimism in, 61; overall argument in, 57; overall constructive feedback in, 60–61; overall questions in, 58; praise in, 57–58; primary audience awareness in, 57, 59, 61–62; punctuation in, 64; questions in, 58–60; relevance in, 62; transitions in, 62; underdevelopment in, 63
common cycles of writing, 34, *35*
common feedback cycle of writing, 34, *35*
compartmentalization, 9
Connors, Robert J., 5–6, *6*, 68
constructive feedback, 60–64
content, 29, 139; in audio commentary, case study #1, 101,

107; in audio commentary, case study #2, 110, 112–13; of case study, English composition final draft, 166–67
content and conventions, *39*, 48, *48*, 150
contradictory comments, xi
controlling comments. *See* directive comments
conventions, *39*, 48, *48*, 139, 150; in audio commentary, case study #1, 107; in audio commentary, case study #2, 111, 113; in case study, English composition half-draft, 159; of case study, English composition final draft, 167
conventions comments: in case study final draft reflection, 168; in commenting vocabulary description, 64–65
copy editing, 50, 64
Corbet, 5–6, *6*
criterion-referenced, 152
CS. *See* comma splice

D2L. *See* Desire to Learn
debatable topic, *77*, 77–78, 79
declarative knowledge, 152
Desire to Learn (D2L), 10–11, 94
diagnostic role, 151
dialogic writing, 151
DID acronym, 54
directive comments: facilitative comments compared to, 30–31, 33–34; sample drafts of, 31–33, *32–33*
dissonance, 151
Draw attention; Identify; Describe (DID acronym), 54
Duncan, Natalia, 132–35

editing logs, 67, 139, 145
editing *Word* file, 65
Edutopia.org, 25
effective comments: content in, 29; direction and facilitation in, 29; encouragement in, 30; functions and qualities of, 28; opportunities in, 30; prioritizing in, 30; process in, 29
EI. *See* emotional intelligence
Elbow, Peter, 49
emotional component, 115–35; addressing, 116; affective domain and, 116; AUP in, 130, *130–31*, 131; biases in, 120–21; emotional weight in, 118; experience of, 119–20; expression of, 116; of feedback process, 117–21; frustration in, 119; grades and, 115, 117, 119, 120; instructors' emotions in, 116, 118, 124–27; intentions in, 119; investment and, 116; issue of, 118–19; miscommunication in, 117; nurturance in, 117; power relations in, 115, 117–18; research on, 120–21; reset buttons in, 121; risks in, 117; role of trust in, 119–20; self-perception in, 118; sentence-level issues and, 119; stages of grief in, 118; student reactions in, *121*, 121–24; tone and diction in, 118; two-way feedback approach and, 118–19; understanding in, 117–18, 119; vulnerability in, 117
emotional intelligence (EI): classroom application of, 132–35; classroom scenario 1 on, 133–34; classroom scenario 2 on, 134–35;

"Common Application Essay" in, 133; cooling-off period and, 128, *128*; definition of, 127; emotions as data and, 129; gratitude in, 133; grit development in, 134–35; instructors' reactions and, 127; links in, 133; before 1:1 conference, 127; 1:1 conference and, 129–30, *131*; questions/statements related to, 130; rapport in, 134; reflection period in, 135; relationship in, 134; scientists compared to judges and, 129, 135; "send" button response and, 128; students' reactions and, 127–29, *128*; teachable moments and, 128, 130; teamwork in, 133; trust in, 133, 134–35; vocabulary list for, 132

encouragement, 38, 96, 140; in audio commentary, 95; in effective comments, 30. *See also* praise

English as standard, 156. *See also* case study, English composition final draft

essay, *170*

essay exam, 34

evaluation, 26, 151. *See also* grades

evidence, 36, *39*, 58–60, 63, *170*; in case study, final draft, 161–63

exigence, 151

expansion, 36, 104, 161, 167

expectations, *35*, 51, 61, 102–3, 105, 150

facilitative comments, 30–31, 33–34

feedback, 151. *See also* specific topics

feedback on feedback: approaches to, 140–41; conventions in, 139; co-regulation of, 137–38, 140; encourage revision risks in, 140; feedback for yourself as, 137; internalization of, 138; not useful comments in, 146; reflection as, 137; rhetorical situation and content in, 139; rubrics on, 139; self-regulation as, 137–38; self-regulation inhibition of, 138; self-regulation teaching methods in, 138–39; self-regulation traits and, 141; student engagement in, 140; students' positive comments in, 146; surveys on, 139; too many comments in, 145–46; "troubled" paragraph in, 140; two parts of, 137

feedback process: academic voices in, 7; alignment in, 10; amount in, 10; audiences in, 6–7; communication in, 10–11; emotional component in, 3; fairness in, 11; feedback description in, 1; framework of, 5–6, *6*; frequency in, 10; general principles of, 4–5; goals in, 4; grades in, 3; guiding questions in, 2, 12; instructors in, 3–4; Kübler-Ross Model of Grief Stages and, 9; "less is more" in, 2; motivation from, 1; openness to, 3; after returning papers, *128*; revision opportunities in, 2; rhetorical triangle in, 6, *6*; successes in, 11–12; time related to, 2, 11, 12; trust in, 1

feedback process premises, 2–3

feed forward, 143–51; benefits of, 144; in classroom, 144; description of, 143; editing log and, 145; feedback on feedback

surveys in, 146–47; guiding questions in, 150; instruction and learning impacts of, 145–47; large classes and, *148*, 148–49; "less is more" in, 149; overall conclusions in, 149–50; "paper load" management in, *148*, 148–49; Pollari on, 143; transfer in, 147
"feed-forward" strategies, xiv
final draft, research paper, 175–78
final draft, rubric for grading, 179
final drafts, 31–33, *32–33*, 51, 67–68, 100. *See also* rough and final drafts
first class survey, 36–37
focus, *32*, 83, 84, 86, 87
formal assessments, 27
formative assessments, 152; on conclusion, 37; description of, 27; effectiveness of, 27; encouragement in, 38; ideal feedback cycle of writing in, *35*; ideal writing cycle in, 34, *35*; quote sandwiches in, 37; rubrics and, 43; summative assessment compared to, 26
fused sentence (FS), 72

grades, 3, *44*, 51, 52, 67, 153; emotional component and, 115, 117, 119, 120
grading rubric, 179
grammar, 64–65
grammar mistakes, 99, *99*
grief, stages of, 9, 118
guiding questions, 2, 12, 18, 150

half-draft case study. *See* case study, half-draft

Hattie, John, xi, 1
heroes, 82–83
history course. *See* case study, research paper
holistic rubrics, 41
humanities, 42

ideal writing cycle, 34, *35*
identity triggers, 122
ineffective assessment criteria: confusion from, 28; contradictions from, 28; control in, 29; negative tones in, 29; perfection and, 29
ineffective comments: damage from, 28; examples of, 30; functions and qualities of, 28; unkindness in, 30. *See also* directive comments
informal assessment, 25; formal assessment compared to, 27
instructors: acceptance of, *8*, 9; anger of, *8*, 9; bargaining by, *8*, 9; belief of, 1; concerns of, 4; copy editing by, 64; denial of, 9; depression of, *8*, 9; frustrations of, 7, *8*; management by, 9; ownership of, xii; from past, 36–37; questions for, 12; roles of, 3–4; supervisors of, 11; time consumption of, xii, xiv, 7, *8*; view of, 3
instructors' emotions, *8*, 9, 116; betrayal in, 124; common emotions in, 118; constructive comments and, 125; destructive comments and, 125; plagiarism related to, 124–25; praise and, 125–27; trust-building in, 125; unhelpful approaches related to, 125

interlinear comments, 152
inter-rater reliability, 41
introduction, *39*

Jimison, Jonny, *8*

Kübler-Ross Model of Grief Stages, 9

large classes, *148*, 148–49
Levi, Antonia J., 41
Lunsford, Andrea, 68

MA. *See* missing or misplaced apostrophe
Mayer, 127
McGee, Patty, 137
MCIE. *See* missing comma after introductory element
meta-analysis studies, xi
metacognition, 152
metacognitive skills, 141
mismatched intentions and perceptions, xi–xii
misperceptions, 123–24, 132, 147
missing comma after introductory element (MCIE), 69
missing or misplaced apostrophe (MA), 70
misunderstandings, xii–xiii, *98*, *99*, 146, 150
"Mother Tongue" (Tan), 157
myths, 82–83

noncontrolling comments. *See* facilitative comments
nonfiction persuasive paper, 99, *99*, 100
norm-referenced, 152
numbered paragraphs, 93, 95

objectives, 13, 14, 50, 90
1:1 conference, 116, 122, 124, 127, 129, 130, *131*
online technology, 95
open-ended question, 36–37
opposing audience, 62

"paper load" management, *148*, 148–49
passive voice (PV), 123, 175, 177, *178*; in case study, research paper rough draft, 170, 171, *171*, *174*
patterns, 75–76
patterns and three-step approach, 65–66
patterns/errors, 65
peer editing, 67
Penaflorida, 73
performance scale for short reflection paper, 48, *48*
personal experience, 163–64
personal pronoun reference vagueness (P Ref), 69
persuasive writing, xiv, 97–98
plagiarism, 124–25
platforms, xiv
Pollari, Pirjo, 143
praise, *174*, *178*, 180; in commenting vocabulary description, 57–58; instructors' emotions and, 125–27
P Ref. *See* personal pronoun reference vagueness
primary audience awareness, 57, 59, 61–62
primary audience awareness constructive feedback, 61–62
primary audience awareness questions, 59

primary audiences, 5, 16, 17, *39*, 51, 57, 59, 61–62, 65
Prn. *See* pronoun
procedural knowledge, 152
prompts, 19, 31, 102, 108, 110, 154, 160, 169
pronoun (Prn), 71
punctuation, 36, *48*, 64, 68, 70, 72, 75, 145; in audio commentary in case study #1, 106, 107
PV. *See* passive voice

questions, 2, 12, 150; analysis in, 60; assessments related to, 25; audio commentary and, 92; in commenting vocabulary description, 58–60; EI related to, 130; evidence in, 59–60; message or thesis in, 59; open-ended, 36–37; overall, 58; primary audience awareness in, 59
quotes, *48*, 76, 102, 103, 104
quotes and paraphrases, 167, 168
quote sandwiches, 37, 75, 76

"Rashomon effect," *84–85*, 84–87
references, 152. *See also* citations
reflection, 48, *48*, 107–8, 113, 135, 137, 139. *See also* case study, research paper final draft online comments
repetitions, 37, 93, 94, 159; in audio commentary, case study #2, 110, 112–13; in case study, research paper rough draft, 171, *174*
reverse/resequence, 11
revision opportunities, 2, *97*
rhetoric, 5–6, *6*, 17, 152, 166
rhetorical argument analysis, 38

rhetorical principles, xiii
rhetorical situation and content, 139
rhetorical triangle, 6, *6*
rough and final drafts: audience in, 85, *85*; comments effectiveness for, 87; focus in, 84, 86, 87; move off topic in, 85; rationale extension for, 85, *85*; too many themes in, 84, *84*; voice in, 85, 87. *See also* case study, English composition final draft; case study, research paper; case study, research paper rough draft
rough draft, 31–32
rough draft, research paper, *170–71*, 170–74, *174*
rubrics, xiv, 16, *39*, 46–48, *48*, 139, 152; characteristics of, 42–43; definition of, 41; descriptions in, 42; dimensions in, 42; on feedback on feedback, 139; feedback related to, 41; formative assessment and, 43; in humanities, 42; nonfiction elements related to, 43; performance indicators and, 44; performance scales and, *44*; pitfalls of, 43; purpose of, 44–45; scales in, 42; summative assessment and, 43; timing of, 42, 44

Salovey, 127
sample draft comments: accusation in, *32*; focus on details, *32*; imbalance in, *32–33*, 33; intolerance on, *32–33*, 33; ownership in, *32–33*, 33; prompt in, 31

sample rubrics: holistic for research proposal, 45–47; performance scale for short reflection paper, 48, *48*
sample rubric with performance scales, *39*
sample writing assignment #1: assignment for, 19; assignment overview on, 18–19; background for, 19; prompt for, 19; sample problem for, 19–20; terminology in, 19
schematic knowledge, 152
school safety movement. *See* case study, research paper rough draft
secondary audiences, 6–7, 17
self-editors, 64, 65
self-referenced, 152
self-regulation, 137–41
sentence-level corrective comments, xii, 64
sentence-level exercise, 67–68
sentence-level issues, 50, 52, 81, 104–5, 119, 167, 168
short story analysis, *78–79*, *97*, 99
social construction theory, 81–82
social media, 16
sociocultural, 152
spelling, 55–56
stages of grief, 9, 118
Star Wars, 82–83
Stevens, Dannelle D., 41
strategic knowledge, 152
strengths, writing, 36
student reactions: acronyms related to, 123; anger as, 123, 131; blame in, 122; confusion in, 123, 132; continuum tool in, *121*, 122; exercise for, 123–24; identity triggers in, 122; intentions and perceptions in, 123–24; misperceptions in, 123–24, 132, 147; not addressing feedback as, 131–32; relationship triggers in, 122; self-critical behavior in, 122; self-esteem in, 126; self-evaluation in, 126–27; self-protection in, 125–26; truth triggers in, 121; validation of, 122, 123; vocabulary in, 123; vocabulary list of, 132
students: concerns of, 4; emotional responses of, xiv; as self-editors, 64, 65; view of, 3
students' ally, 49
students' perceptions, *97*, *98*; confusion in, *78*, 79, *79*; intentions and, *77*, 77–78; understanding in, *77*, *79*, 180
stylistic choices, 152
subject-verb agreement (S-V Ag), 71
summative assessments, 152; formative assessment compared to, 26; rhetorical argument analysis in, 38; rubrics and, 43; sample rubric with performance scales, *39*
summative comments, 9
supervisors, 11
surveys, 36–37, 139, 146–47, 181–82
S-V Ag. *See* subject-verb agreement

Tan, Amy, 157–58, 164
target audiences. *See* primary audiences
taxonomies: in audio commentary, 96–99, *97*, 100–101; on debatable topic, *77*, 77–78, *79*; effectiveness of, 96; implicit

compared to explicit on, 79, 100; method for, 96–97; on a reading, 79, *79*; on short story analysis, *78–79*; students' perceptions related to, 77, 77–78, *78*, 79, *79*; subtext about, 79
teachers. *See* instructors
templates, 95–96, 101
terminal commentary, 152
terms of performance scales, *44*
themes, 84, *84*, 161
thesis, 36, 58–59, 62; in audio commentary, case study #1, 104, 107; in audio commentary, case study #2, 110, 112–13; in case study, English composition final draft, 160, 166
thesis statements, *39*, 76
time, xii, xiv, 7, *8*, 147, 148; for audio commentary, 100–101; feedback process related to, 2, 11, 12
tone, 29, 118; in audio commentary, 90–91, *97*, 98
topic sentences, 76, 80
tough tones, 90
transcripts, audio comments, 103–5, 110–11
transitions, 36, *48*, 65
trust, 1, 119–20, 133, 134–35
trust-building, 125, 129
truth perceptions, 84–85, *84–85*
truth triggers, 121
20 most common student errors: CS in, 70; FS in, 72; its/it's in, 72; MA in, 70; P Ref in, 69, 71; S-V Ag in, 71; UCRE in, 72; VE in, 70; WW in, 69
types of knowledge, 152

UCRE. *See* unnecessary comma(s) with restrictive element
understanding: of audio commentary, 92, 93; in emotional component, 117–18, 119; in students' perceptions, 77, *79*, 180. *See also* assess, understand, and plan approach
University of Michigan, 89
unnecessary comma(s) with restrictive element (UCRE), 72
The Usual Suspects, *84–85*, *84–87*

VE. *See* wrong or missing verb ending
verb form (VF), 71
verb specificity, 56
VF. *See* verb form
vocabulary: expansion of, 36; written commentary on, 75. *See also* commenting vocabulary
voices, 7, 85, 87, 159; in audio commentary, case study #2, 111, 113. *See also* passive voice

webfolios, 152
who, what, when, where, why, 101, 108, 154, 160, 169; in blog posts, 81; in rough and final drafts, 84; in rough draft, 31–32
writing assignments: audiences in, 15–16, 17; avoidances in, 15; fundamental objectives of, 13; guiding question on, 18; invention worksheet for, 17–18; objectives in, 14; proposal sources for, 18. *See also* sample writing assignment #1
written audio commentary, 92, 93, 94

written commentary: alignment of, 74; audio commentary, case study #1 compared to, 107; on blog posts, 80–83; components of, 73–74; on conclusion, 75; goal of, 73; handwritten compared to typed, 73; less as more in, 73; patterns in, 75–76; problems related to, 74; on punctuation, 75; on quote sandwiches, 75, 76; resentment of, 74; revision alternative words in, 74; on rough and final drafts, *84–85*, 84–87; strengths and needs in, 75; in virtual classrooms, 74; on vocabulary, 75

written commentary taxonomies, *77*, 77–79, *78*, *79*

wrong or missing verb ending (VE), 70

wrong word (WW), 69

About the Author

Karen Wink, PhD, is an English professor at the U.S. Coast Guard Academy, where she has taught freshman composition and literature, as well as upper-class world literature courses, for twenty-two years. She earned her doctorate in English education from the University of Maryland and taught high school English in the Howard County, Maryland, school district for four years. Wink received an Excellence in Teaching award from the New England Association of Teachers of English. Her research interests focus on pedagogy in the areas of rhetoric, composition, Shakespeare, and commentary practices in the field of English education.

www.ingramcontent.com/pod-product-compliance
Lightning Source LLC
Chambersburg PA
CBHW030121240426
43673CB00041B/1355